With God in E
chosen word w
in the truest sen.. .. ..d and Spirit. One of my favorite moments is when the author, a soul-care practitioner, invites her readers to craft a thank-you letter to Jesus for our bodies and how they help us on the journey of following him. How original! And so needed for followers of Jesus around the globe. We are not disembodied souls but rather humans, designed to sense our Creator, our deepest needs, those of our neighbors, and every astonishing bit of the world. Here's a book artfully designed to help you in this good work and play. Seize the gift.

Charlie Peacock, Grammy Award–winning music producer, author of *Roots & Rhythm,* and coauthor of *Why Everything That Doesn't Matter, Matters So Much*

Our culture can carve us up into pieces: body, mind, heart, spirit. And sadly, the church often asks us to make choices between these parts of ourselves in how we pursue God. But Scripture sees the human as a whole being and invites us to pursue God with all that we are. Whitney Simpson's work will heal those divides, giving us permission to find God with our whole selves again.

Mandy Smith, pastor and author of *Confessions of an Amateur Saint*

Whitney Simpson is a spiritual director, a yoga instructor, and a podcast host—but what qualifies her to write this beautiful book is that she has experienced deep pain in her own life. The book is not theoretical. It grows out of the author's personal encounters with God and with finding transformational peace through breath prayer and guided meditation. She invites us to join her on the journey through reflections on Scripture from *The Message* Bible. The book will be a treasure for me to cherish for years to come.

Alice Fryling, spiritual director and author of *Aging Faithfully*

After years of practice, Whitney Simpson is a faithful guide, introducing and leading readers in life-giving embodied practices that calm the mind, still the body, and comfort the soul. Through simple breathing, prayer exercises, and thoughtful reflections on Scripture, Simpson invites us on a personal journey to receive the peace of God that surpasses all understanding.

    Sam Gutierrez, associate director of the Eugene Peterson Center for Christian Imagination

In Whitney's signature voice, you are invited to take a much-needed deep breath with a cherished friend. The best part? Whitney reminds us that we already have everything we need to meet God . . . wherever we are. With tools for everyone, she's inviting us to claim what's already ours: spiritual practices that heal our bodies and minds, making a clear path forward and inward.

    J. Dana Trent, author of *Between Two Trailers*

I love *everything* about this book! *With God in Every Breath* engages many aspects of our humanness—the body, the senses, and the imagination—that are traditionally neglected in many contemporary Christian books. Each meditation is spacious and yet simple; holistic and specific; multisensory and deeply thoughtful. Having known Whitney Simpson for many years, I can hear her voice on each page welcoming you, the reader, into this "with-God" life of grounded presence. You will find her book a pleasure to read and a gift to practice!

    Beth A. Booram, spiritual director, cofounder of Fall Creek Abbey, and author and coauthor of several books, including *Starting Something New, Awaken Your Senses,* and *When Faith Becomes Sight*

with God in every breath

A GUIDE TO
DRAWING CLOSER TO JESUS
THROUGH YOUR SENSES

Whitney R. Simpson

NavPress

Published in alliance with Tyndale House Publishers

NavPress
Bold. Loving. Sensible.

NavPress.com

With God in Every Breath: A Guide to Drawing Closer to Jesus through Your Senses

Copyright © 2025 by Whitney R. Simpson. All rights reserved.

A NavPress resource published in alliance with Tyndale House Publishers

NavPress is a registered trademark of NavPress, The Navigators, Colorado Springs, CO. The NavPress logo is a trademark of NavPress, The Navigators, Colorado Springs, CO. *Tyndale* is a registered trademark of Tyndale House Ministries. Absence of ® in connection with marks of NavPress or other parties does not indicate an absence of registration of those marks.

The Team:
David Zimmerman, Publisher; Deborah Sáenz, Acquisitions Editor; Elizabeth Schroll, Copyeditor; Lacie Phillips, Production Assistant; Ron C. Kaufmann and Sarah Susan Richardson, Designers; Sarah Ocenasek, Proofreading Coordinator

Cover illustration of cylinder shape copyright © Iuliia Kundova/Depositphotos. All rights reserved. Cover illustration of geometric flower copyright © Molibdenis-Studio/Shutterstock. All rights reserved.

Interior icons are the property of their respective copyright holders from the Noun Project, and all rights are reserved. Bible © Joy; hand © Kosong Tujuh; nose © Suryaman; mouth © Hary Murdiono JS; ear © visual language; eye © Yudhi Restu Pebriyanto.

Author photo copyright © 2024 by Julia Pearl Photography. All rights reserved.

Unless otherwise indicated, all Scripture quotations are taken from *The Message*, copyright © 1993, 2002, 2018 by Eugene H. Peterson. Used by permission of NavPress. All rights reserved. Represented by Tyndale House Publishers. Scripture quotations marked NIV are taken from the Holy Bible, *New International Version*,® *NIV*.® Copyright © 1973, 1978, 1984, 2011 by Biblica, Inc.® Used by permission. All rights reserved worldwide. Scripture quotations marked NRSV are taken from the New Revised Standard Version Bible, copyright © 1989 National Council of the Churches of Christ in the United States of America. Used by permission. All rights reserved worldwide.

Some of the anecdotal illustrations in this book are true to life and are included with the permission of the persons involved. All other illustrations are composites of real situations, and any resemblance to people living or dead is purely coincidental.

For information about special discounts for bulk purchases, please contact Tyndale House Publishers at csresponse@tyndale.com, or call 1-855-277-9400.

ISBN 978-1-64158-911-6

Printed in the United States of America

31	30	29	28	27	26	25
7	6	5	4	3	2	1

For my mom, Bonnie.

You ignited my passion for books, instilling a deep appreciation for reading, writing, and creating. Even before I could comprehend words on a page, you nurtured my imagination and planted seeds of faith within me.

Your encouragement and support continue to uplift and inspire me today.

Thank you, Mama, for helping me claim my creativity as a gift to share with others.

contents

A Note about Safety *ix*
Introduction *1*
Embodied Living *9*

1 Open Your Eyes *26*
2 Trust in Christ *29*
3 Nourishment from God *33*
4 Simple Pleasures *37*
5 A Holy Vessel *40*

INTERLUDE | WHY *THE MESSAGE* BIBLE?
AN EMBODIED INTERPRETATION *44*

6 See for Yourself *46*
7 Listen and Learn *50*
8 Taste and See *54*
9 Believe and Breathe *58*
10 Cleansed by God's Touch *62*

INTERLUDE | WHAT DOES IT MEAN TO BE WHOLE?
LIVING A "WITH-GOD" LIFE *66*

11 Show the Way *68*
12 Forgiveness and Grace *72*
13 Bittersweet Moments *76*
14 Shared Life Force *80*
15 Hand It Over *84*

INTERLUDE | SAVORING THE SCRIPTURES:
THE PRACTICE OF LECTIO DIVINA *88*

16 Encountering Christ *90*
17 Inner Clarity *93*
18 Partake in the Blessings *96*
19 Wondrous Love *100*
20 New Life *103*

INTERLUDE | CONNECTING WITH GOD:
LIVING LIKE THE CHRISTIAN MYSTICS *106*

21 Looking to Understand *109*
22 Love Others *112*
23 Fed by God *116*
24 Prophetic Presence *119*
25 Held and Changed *123*

INTERLUDE | EMBRACING THE GIFT OF REST:
A COUNTERCULTURAL CALL *126*

26 Radiant Light *128*
27 Simple Calling *132*
28 Forgiveness and Compassion *136*
29 Don't Be Afraid *140*
30 Freely and Lightly *144*

Sensing Our Way Forth *147*

Bonus Content *156*
Acknowledgments *157*
About the Author *160*
Notes *162*

a note about safety

Guided Christian meditation and yoga-inspired movements can be powerful components of a healing journey. The guided meditations in this devotional are offered in the hope you may find them helpful.

The suggestions and practices outlined in this devotional are based on general principles and may not be suitable for every individual. Personalized advice from a qualified healthcare professional and/or a trusted professional therapist, pastor, or spiritual director is recommended.

The use of this book implies your acceptance of this disclaimer.

In this overstimulating world,
as distractions pull me away,
I long to sense your presence.
I pray for the courage to go
slow.

When the world tugs at me,
I remember
I have your breath
in my lungs.

Jesus, the embodiment of God's Spirit,
give me eyes to see
and ears to hear.
Help me sense your presence
this day.

I open my hands
and my heart
now
to taste your goodness.
Your healing touch
is welcome.

Amen.

introduction

God is the still point at my centre.

JULIAN OF NORWICH (CA. 1342–CA. 1416)

Life is filled with storms. It's true. I have had my share, and you have too.

Pause and think of a time when you were physically in a thunderstorm. You know what it feels like to have the house shake or a lightning bolt hit nearby. Consider how the bolts and the bangs feel in your body, how they awaken your senses and shake you to the core.

Lying in an MRI machine on my thirty-first birthday, I felt the storms of life raging around me. Amid the booms and bangs coming from the machine in which I lay, I pondered, *How did I end up here? And how do I find my center?*

Upon awakening early in the predawn of the day with a severe headache, I felt paralyzed on my left side. My left arm and leg were not working as usual. I was very confused. With a toddler in the room next door, I hesitated to wake my dear husband. I fell back asleep, dreaming that this storm had disappeared, but it had not. Amid the confusion I was experiencing, I did finally awaken my family, and we headed to the hospital. That is how I ended up at the emergency room in an MRI machine on my thirty-first birthday.

It took hours to get results, but that MRI showed a mass at the base of my brain, which had caused my paralysis. We were prepared for the fact that doctors thought it was a tumor, and those physicians prepared my spouse and me for the worst outcome. After seizures and many scans, a craniotomy two days later revealed that the mass was a clot from a stroke. There were never clear answers and were many more questions as to how this all happened, but we continued moving forward.

Even without clarity about the cause of my health crisis—amid my confusion and fear—I sensed the presence of God near me. And it was the sweet name of Jesus that I found in prayer that day to calm the storm I was in and center me with my Creator.

The prayer that came to me in the MRI machine was like a whisper during the loudest and most chaotic day of my life: *Jesus, give me peace.*

I prayed that quiet prayer, inhaling *Jesus* and exhaling *give me peace* for hours on end that day and have prayed it many, many more hours since that day two decades ago. Believe it or not, that simple breath prayer calmed my spirit even while I was in the loudest storm of my life thus far. It indeed gave me peace and grounded me when life felt like it was spinning around me.

My birthday health crisis was a near-death experience that awakened my senses as a gift. It was not easy, since that gift also came with many months of chronic pain, medical tests, lifestyle changes, home health nurses, and physical therapy, followed by years of learning new ways to care for my body. And yet, the gift of facing death—and a new way of living—made me more centered, aware, and attentive to the world around me. There are many stories of people coming out of experiences like mine with a new appreciation for life and a new awareness of all that takes place around them. At first, I felt I was overly sensitive from spending so many weeks hospitalized after my stroke. Today, I sense that God gifted me the opportunity to be more connected to the world, the people around me, and the one who created me.

INTRODUCTION

Now, twenty years after my stroke, that breath prayer has become one I turn to often. It became transformational not only for my life but also for my calling and vocation. Now this is my work. I lead others to sense God's presence and to listen with their ears and bodies through ancient practices like lectio divina, breath prayer, and meditation and through mindful movement, like yoga. God has allowed me to work with individuals of various backgrounds, ages, shapes, and sizes and to help them connect their bodies and spirits purposefully—to find their quiet center with God.

This soul care is a type of embodied spirituality for everyone! After all, we all have bodies. Our stories and bodies offer varying degrees of flexibility (literally and figuratively). One factor that causes individuals to hesitate when exploring the body-spirit relationship is how they perceive their physical abilities or bodies. Fortunately, life with Christ is not up to us, our abilities, our bodies, or how we view them.

As people of God, we believe that Jesus is the revelation and the answer for our hurting world. We believe that a Creator bigger than ourselves has a divine plan. We believe that the gift of Jesus does not erase all our troubles but does accompany us in all the storms of life. (I, for one, am glad I do not go through trials alone.) Sometimes, we believe in our heads that God is with us—but do we believe it in our hearts, too? Do we sense that God is truly, really with us now?

For over a decade after my stroke, I was plagued with challenging and chronic health conditions. During an appointment one day, a practitioner asked me a profound (and what I honestly thought at the time to be rude) question. She asked, "Whitney, do you believe you can be well?"

My response was silence (which is rare for this wordsmith). She shocked me, and I couldn't believe she would ask me such a blunt and obvious question. Of course, I wanted to be well; I had taken the time to make an appointment to prioritize my health!

My efforts proved I was working hard at it by investing time, energy, and plenty of financial resources. But did I truly believe that I *could be well*?

Guess what? After my initial shock wore off, I realized I *wanted* to be well but did not *believe* I could be. It did not seem possible that I could live a life free from the pain and anxiety that plagued me after my stroke. And suddenly, as that truth sank in, I began to believe I could be well in a much broader sense than she could have understood. It took some time—months and years—but her words slowly and steadily seeped into my soul. They still do.

Since that question, I have changed my thinking. I do not believe I will always be physically well on this earth (I am human, after all), but I will always be whole in Christ. Yes, we seek guidance for health and wellness from trusted and wise practitioners (I highly recommend it), yet we can only find true healing and wholeness within ourselves from God. (For more reflection on what it means to be whole, see pages 66–67.)

when life is loud, get quiet

It is not uncommon to feel like everything slows down in a crisis, which can make it easier to draw close to your Creator through prayer and petition. I have found that when life returns to full speed, it is easy to lose this connection or longing. Sometimes, we are simply too busy to listen, too busy to look, too busy to sense. We need to slow down long enough to sense the sacred on purpose and get quiet enough to hear what may be only a whisper. But hear me say this: Please do not wait for a crisis to make you pause.

I invite you to pause with me now. Let us draw close to God together.

What if the opportunity to meet God was as close to you as the breath you take every day? What if meeting God engaged all your senses and was a holistic experience for your mind, body, and spirit? What if your experience with God was unique and compared to no one else's? What if sensing the presence of Christ led you toward a more embodied and present life today?

All this is possible.

My breath prayer—*Jesus, give me peace*—is what inspired me to continue exploring the gift of God's peace. Many years later, after much discernment and a shift in career, I began facilitating space for others to connect with God in this way. It was difficult to find resources that invited the imagination and the senses to connect with my Creator that were also grounded in my Christian faith tradition, so I created them. This book you are holding was inspired by my years of experience in leading, facilitating, and enjoying Christ-centered soul care and includes written prayers and guided meditations that you can turn to whenever you need them, for yourself or others. I am honored that you are allowing me to accompany you as we explore guided meditations and prayers in this devotional.

The gift of embodied living invites us to engage our whole selves to connect with our Creator. God came to us in human form, fully human and divine, in the person of Jesus. Using the gifts of our senses and imagination and the experiences of Jesus in the Gospels, we will meet God using Scripture from *The Message* Bible and ask Jesus to guide us in receiving God's healing touch today. This book offers encouraging imagery that will bring clarity and wisdom in your daily life and journey with God.

I love this quote by Henri Nouwen, whose writing has had a profound impact on my journey: "The mystery of one human being is too immense and too profound to be explained by another."[1] This quote reminds us that my journey and yours are not the same and while my story begins this book, your story carries you into these pages. Be reminded that your spiritual-formation journey is unique to you. Try not to compare yourself to anyone else, and instead open yourself up to God in the pages ahead.

open your mind and your heart

> *God is always trying to give good things to us,*
> *but our hands are too full to receive them.*
> ATTRIBUTED TO AUGUSTINE OF HIPPO (354–430)

As we prepare to fully embody God's invitations, I invite you to truly open your mind and release any preconceived notions about meditation that may hold you back. Chances are, if you picked up this book and read this far, you are intrigued by meditation or have experienced the benefits yourself. Study after study shows that meditation offers whole-body benefits.[2]

I did not enter my healing journey as a contemplative, and I did not think yoga and meditation would work for me. I was a skeptic. Two decades later, I cannot fathom my life without these practices. After my stroke, God led me to train as a spiritual director and then as a yoga teacher. And in my work, I have sometimes faced pushback from Christians about embracing embodied spiritual practices like yoga and meditation. People are either too busy to embrace a pause or they do not think the pause will help them find wholeness with God. Some are even skeptical because they believe practices that stemmed from the East, like yoga and meditation, are religions that go against their Christian beliefs. This is not true. Yoga and meditation are indeed spiritual disciplines, but they are not religions themselves. These spiritual practices are accessible to us as Christians, too, and we can embrace them with our intention set on our Creator, God.

I believe that these practices long to meet us in the quiet, no matter what they are called. I am grateful for the profound impact they have made on my body and my spirit. And while I am not a master, I practice because they shape me by quieting my mind and drawing me closer to the one who made me.

Spending time with Jesus helps transform us into being more

INTRODUCTION

like Jesus. Jesus modeled getting quiet for us. He went away to quiet places and listened for and talked with God. We are called to do the same, and Jesus is our perfect companion. I invite you to open your mind and heart as we begin this journey with Jesus together.

Remember, your journey is not mine, nor is it anyone else's. Allow yourself to go slowly through this devotional book and abandon expectations or preconceived ideas.

Thankfully, most Christians today are unafraid to discuss diverse ways of meeting with God. Some of us meet God on a yoga mat, knitting a prayer shawl, walking in nature, or praying over paper with a box of crayons. There is no one-size-fits-all approach! And during various seasons of our lives, our approaches might change. There is no definition for what time apart with our Creator must look like; God invites us to "come away" to a secluded place and rest in his presence (Mark 6:31, NRSV).

What is restful for you on your journey? What times, places, and opportunities have helped you come away and get quiet with God?

I use the word *journey* often in this devotional because that is what we are embarking on together. And as therapist and author Aundi Kolber pens, "Personal growth is a journey, not an event. It's a becoming."[3] So let us enter the becoming as we grow and journey with God through these pages and this experience. We are invited to find rest and "come away" together as we meet God using our whole selves with the companionship of Jesus.

As you open your heart and mind to what is ahead, be reminded that this book is not a replacement for an in-person guide. Your season of life may call for support from a trained spiritual director, counselor, therapist, yoga teacher, somatic coach, retreat leader, or other guide to also accompany you. It is designed to be an introduction to embodied spirituality, a companion to help you meet God in the quiet using your whole self.

The next section of the book, "Embodied Living," will

introduce you to the concepts of imaginative prayer and guided meditation, practices I discovered after my stroke, as well as provide practical tips for your devotional journey. Spend some time absorbing the content, because it will prepare you to engage fully with the meditations that follow. I have also included a few sections throughout the book that will deepen your knowledge and experience of embodied living. Visit these sections at any time and in any order, or return to them when you need encouragement on your embodied journey.

> THIS BOOK IS NOT A STUDY OF GOD'S WORD BUT AN EXPLORATION OF IT.

This book is not a study of God's Word but an exploration of it. It is a whole-body experience designed to be safe and accessible wherever you are on your faith journey. You may have found this book by accident or received it as a gift; we may have journeyed together on a retreat, in a book, or through the *Exploring Peace Meditations* podcast. No matter how you arrived, trust that God has brought you here.

Are you ready?

embodied living

Humanity, take a good look at yourself. Inside, you've got heaven and earth, and all of creation. You're a world—everything is hidden in you.

HILDEGARD OF BINGEN (1098–1179)

Oh, the body. We talk about the body a lot in our culture. We are told what it should eat and drink, how it should look, move, and so on. And while the body does get much attention in our Western culture, it is sadly an emphasis on external focus rather than internal. Celeste Snowber Schroeder writes in *Embodied Prayer*, "The focus is on outer appearance, denying the relationship between the body and heart, mind and soul."[1]

It is true: Your mind and body are extraordinary! God created you with an imagination and senses. God created you to feel, to sense, to be present. God created you to live life fully *with him*. God created you for a "with-God" life! One part of us that is often left behind in Christian churches today seems to be the most obvious—the body. I am passionate about embodied spirituality because God has met me in intimate and healing ways in my very own body. Whether this sentence makes you feel seen or you are confused by what I could mean by "embodied spirituality," this book is for you.

Although our culture often invites us to think about the negative traits of our bodies, I believe our bodies are good and created in the image of our Creator. As W. David O. Taylor reminds us in *A Body of Praise*, "Our physical bodies are not separate or secondary to the divine image that we bear as human beings. They are fundamental to the *imago Dei*."[2] *Imago Dei* means that we are made in the image of God, and that is indeed good news.

Practicing embodiment with God means using the body's sensations to become more aware, remain present, feel whole, love ourselves better, and even get to know our Creator better, the one whose image we are made in. Embodiment practices can help each of us more fully discover the person God created and become more connected to the one who created us—God!

As Christians, this matters because the more connected we are to ourselves and our Creator, the more we can express our God-given longings, needs, gifts, and desires. The body of Christ needs us each to live into our best selves. Can you imagine a world where everyone is connected, grounded, centered, and whole because of their relationship with their Creator? What a gift!

In *Honoring the Body: Meditations on a Christian Practice*, Stephanie Paulsell writes that "the practice of honoring the body is a vital aspect of Christian spirituality. But spirituality is often understood as being made up solely of what individuals do alone, like solitary prayer, meditation, and spiritual reading. And because what is 'spiritual' is often opposed to what is 'bodily,' these activities are often understood as somehow disembodied, as if they engaged the mind and spirit alone."[3] We must not separate what is spiritual from what is bodily. We must bring them together if we long to meet God with our whole selves—body, mind, and spirit.

Hillary McBride reminds us in *The Wisdom of Your Body*, "Embodiment is the conscious knowing of and living as a body, not as a thing distinct from the self or the mind. It is the how, what, why, where, and who of existence—the ground zero of consciousness, of present-moment living. It is to be present to yourself and your experience from the inside out."[4]

Along the way, my journey with embodiment has included gaining a better appreciation and respect for the parts of me that have experienced trauma, negative self-talk, and outright disrespect for the body God gave me. Thank goodness, body positivity is being talked about more and more regarding weight, size, shape, and ability. You may or may not have a positive relationship with the body God gave you at this season of your life. However, you *can* still practice embodied spirituality. You may even find that becoming more embodied gives you more compassion and care for the body God has given you. I am living into this practice each day. I would love for you to come along with me.

On this devotional journey, we practice embodied spirituality and engage the whole self through somatic prompts, imagination, and the mind-body connection. Embodied spirituality is a very personal way to engage with God, yet it is also quite powerful when shared or experienced communally. We are all unique, so my response to an image or passage differs from my neighbor's. Exploring embodied spirituality with others allows us to see and hear things we may not have noticed otherwise and can enrich our spiritual-formation experience. If you long to enrich your experience, consider journeying through the book and these exercises alongside others (perhaps by asking an accountability partner, spiritual friend, or small group to journey with you).

This devotional is an invitation to connect or reconnect with Jesus. And do not be surprised if not all your interactions leave you with peace initially. Some may offer you curiosity, frustration, or even discouragement. After all, Jesus invites our whole selves on this journey.

If your senses or imagination bring up feelings you are not expecting, ask this question often used in spiritual direction: *Where is God in this?* See what arises for you. I will say this again with new words: *Try not to avoid the curious or unexpected when you journey through this book.* Remember, Jesus' life had many highs and lows, and we have opportunities to engage with them all and see what they offer us on our own journeys, which are also filled with highs and lows. Be reminded that if you find yourself accessing unpleasant memories or trauma when you engage your senses and imagination, seek professional companionship from a trained counselor or therapist. Allowing what you are feeling to be processed in your mind and body is a powerful healing opportunity, and it is helpful to have a trusted companion or guide as you learn to listen to the gift of your body.

I have not always considered myself an embodied person. Before my health crisis, I had no concept of what a whole-body experience might look or feel like. Becoming an embodied person is indeed a spiritual practice. Yet if we are mindful and aware, there are plenty of opportunities to be present within our bodies. Additionally, living in a present and embodied way helps us reduce stress, balance the nervous system, decrease experiences of anxiety and depression, and provide a sense of overall well-being.[5]

In ministry, at the intersection of spiritual direction and yoga, I have worked with many people to help them practice embodied living and discover a connection to God through embodied spirituality, from survivors of trafficking to burned-out clergy to college students to kids and senior adults. One thing we have in common is that we all have bodies. And those bodies sense all that is happening around us. If we can learn to live in a more embodied and present way, using our whole selves, we can connect with God no matter our situations, surroundings, or circumstances.

Now, you may wonder how one could have a whole-body experience while reading a book. Connecting with your whole self as you connect with God is a form of embodied spirituality. We go beyond reading for head knowledge. I invite you to read this book as a full-body experience. If that feels outside your comfort zone, that is okay. I hope you will trust me as your companion as we lean into this sensory experience and embrace embodiment as a spiritual practice together.

Using our senses is where we start on this embodied journey of connecting with Jesus as we reach for his healing touch.

the senses

Engaging the senses keeps us present, and *presence is what Jesus is all about*. Just look to the Gospels. *Note:* If some of your senses have diminished or failed, use the senses you have access to as a guide on this journey with Jesus.

Each of the Gospel passages chosen for these reflections makes note of some form of sensory experience. As you read, you will notice an opportunity to connect with Jesus through your body:

- 👁 What is there to see?
- 👂 What is there to hear?
- 👄 What is there to taste?
- 👃 What is there to breathe in?
- ✋ What is there to touch?

Most of us are familiar with our five main senses: *sight*, *sound*, *taste*, *smell*, and *touch*. Some lesser-known senses are harder to explain than these more obvious ones. For example, one class of sensation is known as *exteroception*, which is how we take in information from our surroundings.[6] We also have *interoception* and *proprioception*.

As experiential learning specialist Amanda Blake explains in her book *Your Body Is Your Brain*, "Interoception is essentially the inverse of exteroception"[7] and helps you feel what is happening inside you. Examples of interoception include: Do you

> ENGAGING THE SENSES KEEPS US PRESENT, AND PRESENCE IS WHAT JESUS IS ALL ABOUT.

feel hot, cold, hungry, thirsty, happy, sad, or tired? Interoception helps you notice the emotions that stir in you after you reflect on a passage or a meditation.

Proprioception lets you notice where your body is in space and helps coordinate your movements and sense of balance.[8] For instance, with your eyes closed, you can feel your hands in your lap or arms beside your body without looking to see them there. Proprioception helps you ride a bike or hold this book in your hands as you read.

Using mindfulness, we can engage each of our main senses, as well as exteroception, interoception, and proprioception and live in a more embodied way. After my stroke, I struggled with interoception and proprioception. Embodied living, mindfulness, and much patience have helped me engage these senses again.

Some of us are better at sensing all that is around us than others, and that is okay. I invite you to pause now and notice your body as you read. What do you sense around you in this moment? What sense can you most connect with externally (sight, sound, taste, smell, or touch)? Now allow yourself to connect to what you are sensing on the inside. Ask God to help you notice any internal sensations that arise as you begin this book. Ask God to help you be more present in your devotional time and in your daily life.

The encouraging part is that these reflections go beyond our external senses and bring us inward on our journey with Jesus. They help us practice presence in our lives and with our Creator. You are invited to use all your senses and your whole self along the way.

I invite others to engage the whole self and be in the present moment often. It is a practice I have not mastered for myself; none of us have. Meditation and prayer are called practices for a reason: We return to them again and again and again. And so, with that mindset, we come to these meditations to be present and practice using our senses and imaginations to meet God. If that feels intimidating or overwhelming, take a deep breath, and continue reading when you're ready.

imaginative prayer

> *There is not in the world a kind of life more sweet and delightful than that of a continual conversation with God. Those only can comprehend it who practice and experience it.*
>
> BROTHER LAWRENCE (CA. 1614–1691)

In addition to engaging your senses, you will use your imagination and draw closer to God. Why the imagination? Imagination is a gift from our Creator! We were made to use our imaginations, and this is a resource that is often overlooked or ignored, especially regarding spirituality in the Christian tradition.

Theologian and pastor Gregory Boyd writes, "We might say imagination, when guided by the Holy Spirit and submitted to the authority of Scripture, is our main receptor to the spiritual world. Sadly, the modern Western world has been largely dismissive of this receptor."[9]

What if, rather than dismissing this receptor, we used our imaginations as a tool to connect with God? Might it change the way we pray? Might we find God more accessible to us? This book offers a unique invitation: to meet God, through Jesus, in the Scriptures through prayer, reflection, and imagination. It will help serve as a guide to give you the confidence and companionship you need to meet your Creator with your whole self and allow Scripture to come to life for you in a new and creative way.

Imaginative prayer is not a new concept for Christians. In fact, Saint Ignatius of Loyola (who lived from 1491 to 1556) had a remarkable imagination and was "convinced that God can speak to us as surely through our imagination as through our thoughts and memories."[10] Ignatius taught and led Christ's followers through exercises that engaged their imaginations and often used the Gospels to meet Jesus in his teachings through what he called the Spiritual Exercises.

Praying with our whole selves (imagination, senses, breath,

movement, feelings) is an embodied form of contemplation. Our bodies and brains were designed by God and meant to be accessed. In his book *Meditation for Fidgety Skeptics*, Dan Harris writes, "In recent years, there has been an explosion of research into meditation, which has been shown to reduce blood pressure, boost recovery after the release of the stress hormone cortisol, improve immune system functioning and response, slow age-related atrophy of the brain, [and] mitigate the symptoms of depression and anxiety."[11] While I share this data to show the science, it may be worth noting that Harris was not simply a skeptic of meditation prior to a life-changing experience but is also a self-proclaimed skeptic of God's existence. As with many of the practices of embodied living we will explore in this devotional, some resources do have roots outside Christianity and can also be helpful in our journey to grow closer to Jesus. When we thoughtfully incorporate these into a Scripture-based worldview and lifestyle, we can be less skeptical. If you are a skeptic, lean into the brain science and consider this devotional one that is not only good for your spirit but also good for your whole self. Be present with yourself and your imagination in your quiet time, and you will likely come away feeling refreshed and more connected with your Creator.

guided meditation

Whether or not you have actively practiced any type of formal meditation, you have paused and experienced the benefits. Think about a time you gazed on a beautiful sunset, held a loved one's hand in the quiet, or savored a cup of your favorite warm beverage and genuinely tasted and smelled the experience. Each of these examples is a meditative experience. Our journey will tap into the practice of savoring time apart with God and allowing Jesus to be our guide each step of the way.

People think that because I often (not always) seem (or sound) calm or peaceful, that is my natural inclination. But that is not true. Finding peace takes much practice, and I am grateful I discovered these tools to help me. I need the practices of prayer and meditation in my life.

I began exploring Christian meditation after my health crisis, when I was in my early thirties—twenty years ago. It took me years to settle into my own meditation practice because it was challenging and uncomfortable at first. Oftentimes, it still is!

Many people find meditation intimidating, but it does not need to be intimidating or scary. If prayer is talking to God, meditation is simply quieting our minds and listening to God. And I long to listen to God whenever possible! Here are a few things I've learned over the years:

- *The practice of listening to God through meditation helps us find inner stillness.* We are not striving for anything at all; we are simply resting in God's presence and giving ourselves a break from thinking. Christian meditation does not require an emptying of our minds. Instead, it quiets our minds and helps us rest in God's presence. It is a great way to cultivate peace, self-esteem, clarity, presence, and better relationships.

- *Meditation is beneficial at any time of day.* I find that a morning meditation (silent or guided) sets the tone for my entire day and an afternoon meditation gives me the pick-me-up I need when my energy fades. No matter the time of day, I get to be with God.

- *Meditation can be practiced anywhere.* My meditation practice today does not typically look like sitting on a pillow in the corner of a candlelit room (although that is fun too). I often meditate in my bed, in my car, on my couch, on my yoga mat, while walking, or outside under a tree.

On a recent retreat, after holding space for retreatants and facilitating a time of guided meditation, I asked them to share what it was like to invite Jesus into their quiet meditation time on purpose. Here are some reflections that arose from their sharing:

- "It's like fog on the lake clearing away with the sunrise."
- "It's like a snow globe going from heavily shaken and stirring to calm and settled."
- "It's like Jesus has taken a broom and is helping me clean the cobwebs and dust out of each room of my house (or the corners of my mind)."

What a gift it is to slow down and offer our minds and hearts to God. What a delight it is to have Jesus clear the cobwebs of our minds! Whether new or experienced, you are not alone in your Christian meditation journey: God is our guide, and I am honored to be your companion along the way.

The guided meditations in this book are based on the many meditations I have experienced and led myself. Ideas spark ideas. If there is anything that does not resonate or does not feel comfortable, release it or modify it to meet your needs; this is your journey. Consider making these meditations your own if inspiration arises for you while reading. These words are simply guidance to help you engage your whole self and interact with God, as inspired by the themes in the passages.

We have all experienced different life circumstances. If you find a past trauma or crisis triggered by a passage, invitation, question, or cue, recognize that everything in this book is discretionary. In my training as a trauma-informed yoga instructor, I was taught the importance of options. All prompts, cues, and questions are your option to engage with or not. If something does not resonate, let it go.

It is important to feel your feelings, however. If you feel stirred by something you read or that arises in your imagination, consider exploring that further with a companion. When you recognize a trigger, try not to flee from that sensation; instead, seek support from a trained and trusted counselor, therapist, spiritual director, or pastor.

The sensory cues are designed to be user friendly. If one is not accessible to your body, modify it to meet your needs.

Why is guided meditation good for more than our spirits? Sadly, it is true that today most of us are disembodied and overwhelmed by life. Even those who teach or offer embodied work fall into patterns of disconnecting from our bodies. It is also true that many of us live with some type of trauma, making embodied living even more important in the healing process. Psychologist Dr. Bessel van der Kolk writes in his authoritative and essential book for anyone interested in trauma and the body, *The Body Keeps the Score*, "Trauma victims cannot recover until they become familiar with and befriend the sensations in their bodies."[12] We need to befriend our bodies, becoming more embodied and connected people. Guided meditation can help us, especially when we feel disconnected.

Trauma (big or small) lives in our bodies because it happens all around us.[13] We can choose to disconnect from ourselves or connect with our bodies and engage our spirits, as we invite God into this healing work. It is possible. But it takes practice. This is *your* journey with God; welcome your whole self to it, and see what you learn along the way.

Whether you find it easy or challenging to connect with God, I hope Jesus will come alive to you through these guided meditations and meet you in these pages. Over the years, I have found Jesus to be a practical companion for Christian-guided meditation because we can relate to him as a person. He walked, talked, and lived as a human on this earth. Allowing Jesus to be your companion can help you enter these passages, prayers, and meditations with a friend and embrace guided meditation, especially if it is new or unfamiliar.

These devotions can be done individually or with others. You can use them as your daily quiet time, process them with a spiritual director or therapist, savor them on a retreat, experience them with a small group, or even offer them from the pulpit during worship. *There is no right or wrong way to engage if you enter with an open mind and heart and genuinely long to meet God in your present experience.* Go at your pace, one a day or one a week. The important thing is for you to be consistent and open to meet Christ on your embodied journey, involving your whole self. If you choose one per day, you will notice that there are five days of meditations (one targeted for each sense) and then an "Interlude" section you may choose to read at your pace. If you follow this pattern, this book is a six-week guide.

tips for your devotional journey

Some of my favorite tips for establishing a regular quiet time or meditation practice are as follows.

CHOOSE A TIME: You likely know that consistency is a key factor in creating any routine and sustaining habits. You may have ten minutes in the morning or twenty minutes in the evening to commit to this embodied journey. Start with what works for you, and be consistent. If you recognize that the current time no longer works, pick a new one and stick with it. A daily quiet time best benefits my body and spirit (even if it's brief—consistency is key for me). The time I spend with Jesus varies, but it also adds up. If your schedule varies greatly, consider beginning with a couple of days per week. This is not about legalism; it is about claiming time for yourself and your Creator.

FIND A QUIET PLACE: Choose a quiet place where you will not be interrupted. Finding a quiet place without distractions is not always easy. I have been known to practice meditations like these in my closet, my car, my bed, and my bathroom. You can sit on the floor or in a chair or even lie down and rest in a posture that is calming to you. If you need background sounds to stay present, you can use a meditation app with calming sounds or an instrumental playlist. Remember, you can also put on headphones to block out the world and listen to these meditations by simply scanning the QR code on each page to be taken to that day's guided meditation.

SILENCE YOUR SURROUNDINGS: This feels obvious to say, but sadly it is not: Please turn off the television and silence your phone when journeying with Jesus and your senses through this book. With constant communication, this may be the most challenging tip to embrace. Consider placing your phone on Do Not Disturb mode for the short time you spend with Jesus. Out of habit, I place my phone on Do Not Disturb whenever I open my guided meditations or meditation timer. I am fairly certain that if Jesus sat down in my living room with me today, I would drop my phone immediately to sense his nearness. You may feel that presence and want to snap a selfie with God before your time is up; I understand capturing moments (and if you do, please tag them later with #withGodineverybreath so we can connect)—but for now, just savor God's nearness and release your distractions.

USE AN ANCHOR: An anchor item is something tangible that you can hold or touch while you read or pray. It may be a cross, prayer beads, a stone, your Bible, an icon, your journal, a cup of tea, a hand over your heart, or this very book in your hands! Being purposeful with your anchor item reminds you that you are here to be fully present *with God*, and having an anchor helps remind you when you may be tempted to reach for your phone or task list. Allow your anchor to help you sit with Jesus.

BREATHE: Once you have found a space and released distractions, take a few purposeful deep breaths before reading. Inhale through your nose, expanding your belly as you breathe in. Pause. Then exhale slowly, through your nose or mouth, completely and fully until every ounce of air feels as if it has left your lungs and your belly deflates. Pause again before your next inhale. Focus on your breath for a few rounds and notice how it feels as the breath moves in and out of your body. God created you and gave you breath. Your breath also serves as an anchor and is a foundational starting point for this quiet time of reflecting with Jesus. As noted eloquently by one of my spiritual teachers, Christine Valters Paintner, in *The Wisdom of the Body*, "the breath can also be a tremendous gift in learning how to access and pay attention to body sensations. . . . The breath becomes a tool of awareness and focus for tending to the sensations that arise in the body."[14] I invite you to use the gift of your breath often and let it be a guide into the present.

GO SLOW AND LET GO: Based on the tips I have shared above, this also seems obvious, but it is not easy. Go slow, refrain from multitasking, let go, and be patient. Jesus longs to meet you where you are, and your most important task has already been accomplished: You have chosen to be present with God. Take your time to see what bubbles up during your guided meditation, and if there is nothing beyond the time and space you have made, then that is enough. When your mind wanders (not *if*, because it will wander), acknowledge your thoughts and let them go, then return to your breath, your anchor, and your meditation.

OFFER GRATITUDE: When your guided meditation is complete, take a moment to express gratitude for your time apart with your Creator. Thank God for this moment of stillness and connection for your body, mind, and spirit. Consider a big stretch or give yourself a hug. Dance in gratitude, journal what you have heard, or simply thank God out loud!

We are so close to experiencing these sensations together with God! Are you ready?

Before we dive in, here is an overview of the format of the guided meditations in this devotional book.

SCRIPTURE: Each devotion begins with a passage from *The Message* Gospels. (For more on why I use *The Message* version, see pages 44–45.) As you read, notice the sensory invitations that Jesus and others may have experienced. When you read the passage for each meditation, you may wish to read it more than once in the style of lectio divina (see pages 88–89) or have it audibly read to you using a Bible app. However you read the passage, try to be present with your senses. Rather than reading these words for information, read them formationally and allow them to be the grounding point of your time in meditation.

PONDER THIS: This prompt offers a very simple overview and is not meant to be an all-encompassing theological overview of the Scripture passage. There are entire commentaries written on single passages in this book. The "Ponder" section invites you to wonder about the passage and be curious about what may have been happening for Jesus or others and to consider how this Scripture relates to you today.

GUIDED MEDITATION: Use the meditation tips on the previous few pages for settling into your space, and always begin with a deep breath, then take your time. Pause and place the book down, or simply close your eyes between sections. If you read these meditations for yourself, you will need your eyes to see as you read. Consider pausing and closing your eyes at line breaks to savor what you've read before moving on.

If you prefer to listen to the guided meditations, audio recordings are available via the QR codes located near each one.

If you are leading others through these guided meditations, invite them to close their eyes if that feels safe. If not, have them gaze on an object in the room or soften their gaze, gently allowing their eyes to fall down the tip of the nose. Be sure to pause at the line breaks, allowing the words to sink in for you or the listener.

Your eyes are sensory organs and are an often-overworked part of the body; closing them can help you stay present and pause the receptors that receive loads of information for your brain and body throughout the day.

Note: These meditations are a product of creative imagination and spiritual exploration. As with any meditation, feel free to adapt it to suit your needs. Each meditation is an invitation with guidance meant to enhance your connection to God's Spirit.

SOAK IN SILENCE: Allow yourself a moment of silence to soak in what God is inviting you to notice.

American priest and centering prayer proponent Thomas Keating wrote, "Silence is God's first language; everything else is a poor translation."[15] Consider what happens when you get quiet and truly listen to your body, letting the outside voices fade away and instead sensing God's presence in the quiet. Give yourself permission to stay there and be quiet as long as you are able, honoring the needs of your body and spirit. Be patient with silence, for although challenging for many, it may be the most valuable part of your contemplative journey.

FOR REFLECTION: I end each devotional with reflection prompts that are meant to help you listen to and sense more deeply what you have read, sensed, and experienced. As time allows, you may wish to journal your reflections in this book or in your journal. Or, if you prefer, pause and quietly reflect rather than write. While there is a bonus body-mind connection when you physically write your reflections, there is no right or wrong way to engage with the prompts.

SENSORY CUE: The sensory cues are meant to be gentle and soothing, and most are to be carried into your day, helping you soak in your meditation beyond your quiet time. These prompts invite you into a somatic connection with your guided meditation. *Soma* means "body" in Latin. These sensory cues or somatic invitations are all connected to your physical body and are meant to be accessible to everyone. If you experience any discomfort, pain, or overstimulation in your body at any time, adjust or simply stop the activity. It is important to listen to your body and only engage in sensory activities that feel comfortable for you. If you need to physically modify for your body, take these as suggestions or cues and make the invitations applicable.

CLOSING PRAYER: Offer your own prayer to God or add to the short prayer prompt as you wish. Bring gratitude into each of your reflections, and thank God for anything you may have sensed in the presence of Jesus. Whatever arises, feel it, sense it, or name it before God!

Let us begin as we connect *with God in every breath* through Scripture, meditation, movement, journaling, reflection, and prayer.

1
open your eyes

Read reflectively: Matthew 6:22-23

A Life of God-Worship
[Jesus said,] "Your eyes are windows into your body. If you open your eyes wide in wonder and belief, your body fills up with light. If you live squinty-eyed in greed and distrust, your body is a musty cellar. If you pull the blinds on your windows, what a dark life you will have!"

ponder this

In the Sermon on the Mount, Jesus uses the metaphor of the eyes being the body's windows (or, in other translations, the eye as a lamp) to illustrate how our spiritual perception affects our entire being. Just as our eyes enable us to see the physical world, our spiritual eyes (our perception, understanding, and priorities) determine how we view life and engage in the world around us.

guided meditation

Center yourself in your space by taking a few deep breathsand welcoming God's presence with you. Now bring your gaze to an ordinary object nearby, something you might not typically pay much attention to. It could be a simple household item, an object in nature, or anything your eyes are drawn to in this moment. Gaze on this object before you as you take three to five deep breaths.

Slowly begin noticing the small details of this object, the intricacies that often go unnoticed. See it with fresh eyes, as if encountering it for the first time. Observe its shape, texture, or color.

Take time to explore every aspect, as if unraveling its ordinary yet hidden beauty. What might you see that you have not noticed before?

Now imagine that you are lending your eyes to God, as if you are gazing through a fresh, clean window of perspective.

God's light can reveal new insights and understanding not only in what you see with your physical eyes but also in your life. Pause and invite God into your thoughts, emotions, and experiences. Ask God for open eyes to see.

Say to yourself:

I am open to seeing things with the eyes of God.
I am willing to notice the beauty and divine presence in even the most minor aspects of life.
I see anew today because I see with the eyes of God.

Embrace this practice of holy gazing and gain a fresh perspective that allows you to appreciate the wonders surrounding you in this moment and in everyday life.

soak in silence

Pause in the quiet and breathe purposefully. What do you sense?

for reflection

1. Does the practice of holy gazing allow you to see in new ways?
2. What small details do you sometimes miss?
3. What can you do today to soak up more of God's light and open the windows of your eyes?

sensory cue

Rub your hands together, feel the warmth that is generated, then close your eyes and place your palms over your eye sockets. There should be no pressure from your hands. Offer a blessing for your eyes, and ask God to help you continue to see anew this day. Rest with your eyes closed and palms over your eyes for anywhere from one to ten minutes. Return to the world with fresh eyes and an open mind.

closing prayer

Lord,
Give me fresh eyes to see you, this day and always.
Amen.

2
trust in Christ

Read reflectively: John 14:1-4

The Road

[Jesus said,] "Don't let this rattle you. You trust God, don't you? Trust me. There is plenty of room for you in my Father's home. If that weren't so, would I have told you that I'm on my way to get a room ready for you? And if I'm on my way to get your room ready, I'll come back and get you so you can live where I live. And you already know the road I'm taking."

ponder this

Today's Scripture centers around the assurance of Jesus' presence and comfort and the promise of eternal life. It offers hope and encouragement to us as believers, reminding us of the enduring love and care of Jesus, now and forever. Carry forth these words of Christ in this passage—*Trust me*—as you listen for God in the following meditation.

guided meditation

Visualize yourself in a beautiful, serene meadow. The sun is gently warming your skin, and a soft breeze rustles through the leaves of nearby trees. You step forward and feel the cool, lush grass beneath your feet and between your toes. With each step, you become more aware of the earth supporting you, its positive energy rising through your body.

Imagine safely walking barefoot through this meadow, feeling the blades of grass tickling your feet. As your feet press into the ground, sense the connection between you and the earth, a bond that has existed since the beginning, between you and creation. Picture the energy of God's earth beneath your feet, anchoring you securely.

As you walk, you hear your breath. Listen also to the symphony of nature surrounding you. The songs of birds, the gentle rustling of leaves, and the murmur of a stream comfort you. Allow these sounds to wash over you, calming your mind and filling you with peace and presence in God's creation.

As you engage your imagination to bask in the beauty of the earth and in the rich colors around you, let your thoughts turn to God, the Creator of all things. Feel a sense of awe and gratitude for the beauty and intricacy of the natural world around you. Know that you are part of this magnificent creation!

Say to yourself: *I trust God's guidance in my life.*

Bring your awareness to Jesus standing nearby, your guiding light of love and compassion. Feel Christ's presence beside you, walking with you through this meadow, leading your way. You can almost hear his gentle words of encouragement and understanding, showing you the way along the path. Trust him. Allow his love to wash over you, filling you with a sense of belonging and acceptance, reminding you there is space for you beside him. Bask in this moment with your companion, and feel yourself trust in him completely as he guides you through the meadow.

And as you continue walking, imagine the Holy Spirit as a pleasant, gentle breeze that moves through the meadow with you and Jesus. Listen for the breeze, feel the Holy Spirit's subtle touch, carrying whispers of inspiration and guidance. Allow his wisdom to flow into your heart and mind, bringing clarity and peace.

Stay in the meadow of peace, enjoying nature's symphony as long as you are able. As thoughts arise that take you away, allow them to float down the meadow's stream.

When you are ready to continue your day, ask God's Spirit to come with you to cover and guide you as you do, relishing the peace of this symphony and your trust in Christ.

soak in silence

Pause in the quiet and breathe purposefully. What do you sense?

for reflection

1. Have you ever sensed God asking you to trust him?

2. What does it look like to journey so closely with Jesus that you trust him completely? Have you ever trusted him completely?

3. How might you grow this connection of trust with God in your everyday life?

sensory cue

Find a comfortable space to relax your body, either in a chair or reclining on a couch, bed, or the floor. Soften your shoulders, relax your jaw, and allow the back side of your body to sink and settle into the surface beneath you as you let go. Now trust the surface beneath you as you remain as still as possible in this relaxed state, recognizing the challenge of being still and letting go. Notice what it feels like to be held by God's energy. Remain still for several minutes and continue softening the body with each breath as you relax into God's presence.

closing prayer

Creator,

Help me trust your guidance on the roads of my life. When I cannot discern the next steps, help me listen, let go, and follow you.

Amen.

3

nourishment from God

Read reflectively: John 6:27-33

The Bread of Life
[Jesus told the crowd,] "Don't waste your energy striving for perishable food like that. Work for the food that sticks with you, food that nourishes your lasting life, food the Son of Man provides. He and what he does are guaranteed by God the Father to last."

To that they said, "Well, what do we do then to get in on God's works?"

Jesus said, "Sign on with the One that God has sent. That kind of a commitment gets you in on God's works."

They waffled: "Why don't you give us a clue about who you are, just a hint of what's going on? When we see what's up, we'll commit ourselves. Show us what you can do. Moses fed our ancestors with bread in the desert. It says so in the Scriptures: 'He gave them bread from heaven to eat.'"

Jesus responded, "The real significance of that Scripture is not that Moses gave you bread from heaven but that my Father is right now offering you bread from heaven, the *real* bread. The Bread of God came down out of heaven and is giving life to the world."

ponder this

This passage invites us to consider the distinction between earthly and spiritual sustenance, emphasizing that we are to seek eternal nourishment from our Creator, God. As you enter this time of meditation, ponder the many ways God nourishes you each day.

guided meditation

Imagine yourself in a serene and peaceful space. This can be any place that feels safe and nurturing to you, whether it's a favorite room, a beach, a mountaintop, or a meadow. Visualize this place in as much detail as you can. What does it look like? What colors do you see? Are there any sounds or scents that soothe you? Claim this space as your very own sanctuary. Now welcome the gentle presence of your Creator, God, surrounding you like a warm embrace, offering love and guidance.

In the center of this sanctuary, you see a space to sit or lie down, where you can relax and connect with your inner self and your Creator. Make your way there, and as you do, continue to notice this gentle, soothing presence that envelops you. This energetic embrace represents God's divine presence within you and all around you.

You recognize suddenly that you have a great thirst—you are parched beyond belief—as you feel the energy flow in and through you. And as you lift your gaze, you notice there is a pitcher of water just for you. You drink the water lavishly; it feels lifesaving. It quenches every thirst you've ever had and feels nourishing to your body and spirit. Each sip you take promises new life.

Take a moment to express gratitude for God satiating you beyond this pitcher of water, for being in this sacred space, and for giving you the gift of connecting with your Creator. Bask in the presence of God. Feel the unconditional love and acceptance not only filling you but also surrounding you.

As you rest in this inner sanctuary, practice this breath prayer silently or aloud:

(inhale) *Creator-God,*
(exhale) *nourish me.*

Remain in this inner sanctuary as long as you are able, breathing and praying, feeling a renewed sense of refreshment, peace, and strength only offered by the one who nourishes and sustains you.

soak in silence

Pause in the quiet and breathe purposefully. What do you sense?

for reflection

1. Are you feeling nourished and satiated in your spiritual life?

2. If God is the bread that fills you and the water that quenches you, are you hungry or thirsty today?

3. If you are not satisfied, ask God, *What is missing in my life?*

sensory cue

As your health allows, consider fasting from a meal this week or abstaining from a certain food or beverage to increase your need for God's nourishment and deepen your spiritual connection with him. Notice the sensation of hunger or thirst within you as you ponder the difference between physical and spiritual hunger.

closing prayer

God,
Nourish me as only you can. I long to be satisfied by you and you alone.
Amen.

4
simple pleasures

Read reflectively: Luke 17:20-21

When the Son of Man Arrives
Jesus, grilled by the Pharisees on when the kingdom of God would come, answered, "The kingdom of God doesn't come by counting the days on the calendar. Nor when someone says, 'Look here!' or, 'There it is!' And why? Because God's kingdom is already among you."

ponder this

The Kingdom of God is not a place in the clouds but a spiritual reality in the lives of those who journey with God. May we be encouraged to seek the presence of the Kingdom in our hearts and lives in the here and now.

guided meditation

Take a few deep, cleansing breaths to center yourself in this moment. Allow your chest and belly to rise and fall. Notice the sensations as your lungs expand and deflate. Allow any thoughts to be present without judgment. You are here now; exhale a big sigh of relief.

Ponder blessings in your life. Reflect on the people, experiences, and things that bring you joy and gratitude. Consider the faces of those you are grateful for and the material things that help you feel stability and peace. These are gifts that God has bestowed on you; pause and breathe as you savor them.

As you inhale, think about some simple pleasures in your life that often go unnoticed—this breath in your lungs, the wind on your face, or the smell of a favorite meal. Feel thankful for these small, unique moments, these simple pleasures.

With each breath, acknowledge the presence of the divine in the now. Offer a prayer to Jesus, talking to him like a friend in this moment of quiet.

Take a few moments in silence to allow any additional thoughts, feelings, or expressions of gratitude to arise. Feel the sensation of your breath as you remain present.

Say, *Thank you, God, for the pleasures of the here and now.*

Noticing the simple pleasures of life is a practice, and it can be cultivated with time and consistency. Return to this meditation whenever you need a reminder of the blessings in your life and the presence of God in the now—right now.

Far from simple, Holy Spirit, your breath in me helps me realize the Kingdom is within me, as close as my breath.

soak in silence

Pause in the quiet and breathe purposefully. What do you sense?

for reflection

1. What are some simple blessings or joys you have received or experienced recently?

2. Can you imagine God's Kingdom with you now, beginning with your breath?

3. How can you practice breathing in appreciation for God's ongoing presence in your life?

sensory cue

Practice box breathing today as a reminder of God's steady presence with you. Slowly inhale for a count of four, hold the breath steady for a count of four at the inhale, gently exhale for a count of four, and hold the breath steady for a count of four at the exhale. Repeat your box breath for a few rounds or up to a few minutes, increasing as it feels comfortable. If you find it helpful, trace a box in your mind's eye as you breathe.

closing prayer

God,
May I feel you as close as my own breath.
Amen.

5

a holy vessel

Read reflectively: Mark 5:21-24

A Risk of Faith
After Jesus crossed over by boat, a large crowd met him at the seaside. One of the meeting-place leaders named Jairus came. When he saw Jesus, he fell to his knees, beside himself as he begged, "My dear daughter is at death's door. Come and lay hands on her so she will get well and live." Jesus went with him, the whole crowd tagging along, pushing and jostling him.

ponder this

Faith and desperation led a father to ask Jesus to heal his daughter. Willingness to fall down and beg for Jesus' touch was a risk this man took to save his daughter. Consider the many who followed Jesus and sought his healing touch in their lives.

guided meditation

Pause and reflect on the sacred nature of the body. Your body is a miracle of God's creation. It is a holy vessel through which you experience the world. Savor this gift for a moment as you breathe, fully and deeply.

Now turn your attention to honoring your body. Feel a deep sense of gratitude for all that it does for you. Allow gratitude to move from the top of your head to the bottom of your toes. As you scan down your body, gently lay your hand on your heart, expressing gratitude for your whole self.

Feel gratitude for how your body carries you through each day, allowing you to experience life's joys and challenges. This divine creation, your body, is home to your soul. From this centered place, pause to offer your body words of humble appreciation, silently or aloud, as you thank God for the gift of this sacred vessel you live in!

From gratitude, we move to respect as the next step on this journey. Pause now and listen closely to your body's needs, for it holds wisdom that is uniquely yours. What does your body need in this season? Can you ask your body this question and offer it to God?

Tune in to the longings of your body as you breathe and respond to what you hear with love and compassion.

Say to yourself: *My body is a miracle. I will treat my body with the kindness and respect it deserves.*

Take a full inhale and a long exhale with an audible sigh. Notice a renewed sense of purpose and commitment to caring for your body as a sacred vessel, and beg Jesus to accompany you.

soak in silence

Pause in the quiet and breathe purposefully. What do you sense?

for reflection

1. How has your body faithfully served you?
2. How do you prioritize caring for your physical body?
3. Do you have faith in the vessel God created for you?

sensory cue

Use your fingertips or lightly clenched fists for this abbreviated tapping-relaxation exercise that opens you to the wonders of your body.

Begin by tapping gently on the tops of your shoulders. Move your tapping from your shoulders to across your collarbones, right below your neck. Aim for a comfortable level of pressure that feels soothing rather than painful. You can tap with both hands simultaneously or alternate between each side of the body. You can experiment with different patterns, such as light, rapid, slower, or deeper taps. Try to sync your tapping with your breath, finding a pace that feels most calming and comforting to you.

Focus your attention on the sensations created by the tapping as you breathe. Notice the gentle vibrations spreading through your body and the warmth generated by the tapping motion. Say to yourself, *I release any tension and tightness in this body, my sacred vessel.* Take a moment to sit quietly, observing the relaxed sensation in your shoulders and collarbones. Notice any openness or refreshment this touch has brought you. Return to this tapping relaxation activity when you need to feel refreshed.

closing prayer

Faithful One,

Please guide me in caring for the body you have given me. Offer your healing touch upon me this day.

Amen.

Interlude
why *The Message* Bible?
An Embodied Interpretation

While I have many Bibles on my shelf, *The Message* is my most worn-out translation.

I grew up in a tradition that helped me appreciate Scripture, but I did not always understand how it applied to my life until I read *The Message* Bible as an adult. My sister gifted me a copy after my stroke, and it has become a close companion for many reasons. First and foremost, the translator, Eugene Peterson, uses words and phrases that are easy to understand in this culture, showing that God's Word is relatable and understandable. Second, *The Message* is the most embodied translation of the Bible. The sensory language that Peterson uses in this translation invites us to feel, sense, and understand what God's people in it experienced.

In this book, I focus each devotion and meditation around a Gospel reading from *The Message*. The Gospels tell the story of Jesus, and Jesus is God's embodied gift to us! He is the perfect guide and companion for embodied meditations.

The four Gospel writers documented these stories about Jesus from varied perspectives, oftentimes noticing different aspects of the same stories. As you reflect on the Scripture passages that accompany the guided meditations, I invite you to pay attention to what you notice along the way. These stories offer tangible experiences that many of us can relate to today. If you allow it, you will find that *The Message* Bible translation offers an embodied interpretation that will make these stories and parables come to life.

Talking about Scripture (and the Psalms specifically), Peterson once said that when he discovered metaphors and passages beyond the literal meaning, Scripture opened up to him in a new way, and he learned that "imagination was a way to get inside the truth."[1] Peterson met and discovered God in new ways using his imagination, and I hope this book will help you do the same.

In 2016, Eugene Peterson recorded a documentary short film with musician and activist Bono in which they discussed *The Message*, focusing on the Psalms. They talked specifically about the emotions the Scriptures evoke in them. Bono was recorded saying that we need to live more authentically with our feelings, urging us to "let them out."[2] Bono is right! God's loving presence is most present with us as we engage with what we notice and let it out rather than stuff it in. When you notice feelings rise as you read through this devotional, pause and feel them. Let them out by journaling, talking to God, or sharing with a spiritual friend about what is bubbling inside you. *This* is embodied living.

That said, feelings are not always easy to uncover or express. In *Pause, Rest, Be: Stillness Practices for Courage in Times of Change*, Octavia F. Raheem notes that feeling itself may even be an act of rebellion "when you've been conditioned to stuff everything in. Overwork and grind it away. Pretend it away. Bypass it away. Joke it away. Pray it away. Fuss and fight it away."[3] What might you have denied, covered up, or prayed away over the years? May you be brave enough to keep reading and open yourself up to what your body offers you within and beyond these pages.

6
see for yourself

Read reflectively: Mark 3:7-10

> *The Twelve Apostles*
> Jesus went off with his disciples to the sea to get away. But a huge crowd from Galilee trailed after them—also from Judea, Jerusalem, Idumea, across the Jordan, and around Tyre and Sidon—swarms of people who had heard the reports and had come to see for themselves. He told his disciples to get a boat ready so he wouldn't be trampled by the crowd. He had healed many people, and now everyone who had something wrong was pushing and shoving to get near and touch him.

ponder this

Those around Jesus see his growing influence. The significance of his ministry is drawing crowds and revealing his impact on people's lives as they come to him with their needs and desires. The crowds long for his healing touch; they want to see his great miracles! This story reminds us of our longing to draw close to Jesus and see for ourselves that he can relieve us of our burdens, our hurts, our worries, our stresses—even today.

guided meditation

For this body scan, begin by finding a quiet and comfortable place to relax without distractions. You may wish to sit or lie down. After you read this guidance, consider closing your eyes to savor your posture of relaxation.

Take a moment to bring your awareness to the present. Invite God to meet you now. Allow yourself to feel seen and embraced by the love and grace of your Creator.

Now gently shift your attention to your body. Start by bringing your awareness to the crown of your head. Notice any sensations, such as warmth, tingling, tightness, or coolness. Be present with these sensations, acknowledging their presence without judgment.

Move your attention slowly down to your forehead, noticing any sensations or tension in this area. If you feel any tightness or pressure, imagine God's healing presence gently releasing and melting away the stress. Allow your forehead to relax. Soften your eyes as you read these words or close them between paragraphs.

Notice the weight of your eyelids. Allow your eyes to relax and let go of any strain or tension.

Shift your attention to your nose. Notice the sensation of the air passing through your nostrils as you breathe in and out. Take a moment to appreciate the gift of breath and the life force flowing through you.

Continue to scan your body with your mind's eye, focusing on your cheeks, jaw, and mouth. Allow these areas to soften, and release any tension or tightness. Notice any sensations in your lips or tongue.

Bring your awareness to your neck and shoulders. As you breathe in, imagine God's healing presence flowing into your neck and shoulders, releasing any tightness or knots. As you breathe out, envision the tension leaving your body, allowing your shoulders to drop and relax.

Move your attention down to your chest and heart area. Notice the rise and fall of your chest with each breath. Soften your entire core, including the organs within you. Allow yourself to sense the presence of God's compassion, care, and love within you.

Now shift your attention to your arms, hands, and fingers. Notice any sensations, such as warmth or coolness. Be present with these sensations.

Bring your awareness to your abdomen and lower back. Notice any sensations or tightness in this area. With each breath, invite God's healing presence to soothe and relax these muscles, allowing any tension to melt away.

Move your attention to your hips, thighs, and legs. Notice the weight of your body on the surface beneath you. Allow your legs to release any tension and surrender to gravity, as if being held by God.

Finally, bring your awareness to your feet and toes. Notice any sensations in these areas. Allow any tension or discomfort to dissolve.

Picture your entire body in your mind. See how relaxed, calm, grounded, and whole it is, thanks to God's healing touch in your life. Envision that your entire being is filled with God's divine love and presence.

Say to yourself: *I am grateful for this body.*

When you are ready, slowly bring your attention back to the present moment. Gently wiggle your fingers and toes, allowing your body to reawaken, and reenter your daily life—released, relaxed, refreshed, healed.

soak in silence

Pause in the quiet and breathe purposefully. What do you sense?

for reflection

1. How does relaxing in God's presence help you see for yourself the wonders of the body and its Creator?
2. As you draw closer to Jesus on this journey, what would you like to see him do for you today?
3. Can you sense God's healing presence in your own body? Do you long for more of it?

sensory cue

A body scan can be practiced regularly to cultivate a more profound sense of presence in God's loving embrace and to develop a greater connection with your body and the present moment. When you notice feeling stressed or tense today, tighten and release the part of your body that feels burdened, and imagine seeing God's healing presence settle on you. Notice any lightness that arises after you release the physical tension in yourself.

closing prayer

Lord,

Help me see you within me and around me. Draw me close to you and your healing touch this day.

Amen.

7
listen and learn

Read reflectively: John 13:10-17

Washing His Disciples' Feet
Jesus said, "If you've had a bath in the morning, you only need your feet washed now and you're clean from head to toe. My concern, you understand, is holiness, not hygiene. So now you're clean. But not every one of you." (He knew who was betraying him. That's why he said, "Not every one of you.") After he had finished washing their feet, he took his robe, put it back on, and went back to his place at the table.

Then he said, "Do you understand what I have done to you? You address me as 'Teacher' and 'Master,' and rightly so. That is what I am. So if I, the Master and Teacher, washed your feet, you must now wash each other's feet. I've laid down a pattern for you. What I've done, you do. I'm only pointing out the obvious. A servant is not ranked above his master; an employee doesn't give orders to the employer. If you understand what I'm telling you, act like it—and live a blessed life."

ponder this

Jesus, the Son of God and the Messiah, washes the feet of his followers as a servant would do. He demonstrates humility, selflessness, and willingness to serve others with this simple and unthinkable act of cleansing their feet. Jesus' actions challenge the conventional notions of power and authority, teaching his followers that true greatness lies in serving others. He also asks a clear question and checks with his followers to see if they heard him. Listen for how God may be speaking to you in the following meditation.

guided meditation

Imagine yourself in a peaceful and serene place, surrounded by the beauty of nature, perhaps sitting on a hill. The air is quiet and still. Listen closely and imagine that you hear gentle rain beginning to fall from the sky. Sense the coolness of each unexpected but welcome raindrop as it touches your skin, bringing with it the sounds of renewal and cleansing. Savor the breeze caressing your body. Listen to the wind gently blowing all around you. Allow your ears to take in every soothing sound, and pause as you breathe.

As the raindrops fall, let them wash away any tension or worries you may carry. Hear the rain fall and visualize the raindrops gently cleansing your entire body and mind, purifying you inside and out.

With each imagined raindrop, feel a sense of release and surrender, and let go of anything that no longer serves you. Allow the rain to wash away any burdens or judgments you may be carrying, leaving you feeling lighter.

As you hear the raindrops puddle, invite a deep sense of humility into your being, inspired by the humility that Jesus teaches us. Recognize that true humility allows us to be open, receptive, and willing to learn and grow. Allow yourself to be free of any barriers that keep you from living like Christ. Take your next three breaths in through your nose and sigh out through your mouth.

Listen to your sighs. Feel the relief.

Imagine that each raindrop that touches your skin carries the essence of Jesus' humility. Feel that essence permeate your entire being, inviting a gentle softening of the ego and a willingness to let go of worldly pride and self-importance. Release another sigh, symbolizing the letting go of these ego traits.

Embrace the sensation of humility as it flows through you, recognizing that it is a strength that allows us to connect more deeply with ourselves, others, and our Creator, God.

As the rain continues to fall, imagine that it not only cleanses your physical body but also purifies your heart and soul. Listen for any lingering doubts, fears, or resentments, and invite them to be washed away by the rain, leaving only a sense of clarity and peace from your Creator.

Take a few moments to fully immerse yourself in the sensation of the raindrops on your skin and the invitation of God's transformative power.

Say to yourself: *I treasure the gentle rain and listen for its symbolism of renewal, cleansing, and humility.*

Slowly bring your awareness back to the present moment.

soak in silence

Pause in the quiet and breathe purposefully. What do you sense?

for reflection

1. How does Jesus' life of service inspire your own? What has he taught you?
2. Is there a human trait that slips you up, that occasionally gets in the way of living a life of humility?
3. What humbling acts of service have you offered others recently?

sensory cue

Move to a sink or practice this exercise the next time you wash your hands. Listen as the water pours out and covers your skin. Imagine Christ washing your hands at this very sink. Carry the meditation forth as the water cleanses your fingers and palms. Sense the water on your skin and offer gratitude for these hands that humbly serve God and others. Finally, hold the cleansing water God is offering you briefly in your cupped hands and ask God for a fresh start. Listen for God's response.

closing prayer

Jesus,
Thank you for teaching me how to live a life of service and humility. Help me listen to you and be a disciple who models your life to others.
Amen.

8
taste and see

Read reflectively: Matthew 5:13-16

Salt and Light

[Jesus said,] "Let me tell you why you are here. You're here to be salt-seasoning that brings out the God-flavors of this earth. If you lose your saltiness, how will people taste godliness? You've lost your usefulness and will end up in the garbage.

"Here's another way to put it: You're here to be light, bringing out the God-colors in the world. God is not a secret to be kept. We're going public with this, as public as a city on a hill. If I make you light-bearers, you don't think I'm going to hide you under a bucket, do you? I'm putting you on a light stand. Now that I've put you there on a hilltop, on a light stand—shine! Keep open house;

be generous with your lives. By opening up to others, you'll prompt people to open up with God, this generous Father in heaven."

ponder this

Salt gives flavor; it enhances and preserves food. Light helps us see and be seen. We are called to be salt and light, to taste and see on this journey with God as we help others savor the goodness of God. As Christ's followers, we are invited to reflect on the characteristics that flavor Jesus' ministry with God's love, compassion, grace, and truth! Open your senses and savor God's presence in your life today.

guided meditation

Bring your attention to the present moment, focusing on your breath. Notice your chest's gentle rise and fall as you breathe in and out. Allow the familiarness of your breath to anchor you right here at this moment.

Now, with only your imagination, shift your attention to your sense of taste. Imagine you are about to embark on a journey of sensory delight, exploring tastes and flavors. Bring to mind a favorite taste that brings you joy.

Visualize that food item in your mind's eye. Imagine its color, texture, taste, and aroma. Let it fill your awareness, cultivating a sense of anticipation and delight as you imagine it. You can pause here and close your eyes to sense the tastes and flavors fully.

As you imagine tasting your favorite food, notice the initial burst of flavor as it touches your taste buds. Is it sweet, bitter, salty, sour, or savory? Take a few moments to enjoy the taste, fully immersing yourself in the sensation. Observe the subtle changes in taste as you imagine chewing, and allow the flavor to unfold.

Next, bring your awareness to the texture of the food. Is it smooth, juicy, or crunchy? Notice how the texture adds to the overall experience and your appreciation for this gift of taste. Express gratitude for this moment of sensory delight. Give thanks for the ability to experience and appreciate the subtleties of taste God offers us.

Recognize that this simple appreciation for flavor can extend to all aspects of your life, cultivating a more profound sense of presence and gratitude.

Say to yourself: *I am grateful for the way my sense of taste allows me to savor not only my favorite foods but also my very life.*

Return to the present as you embrace the richness of all you taste and see.

soak in silence

Pause in the quiet and breathe purposefully. What do you sense?

for reflection

1. Have you ever temporarily lost your sense of taste? How did it change your experience of daily life?
2. What joyful or good things does God want you to notice more closely and savor more deeply?
3. How might you give more flavor and shine more goodness (i.e., be salt and light) in the world around you?

sensory cue

For your next meal, practice mindful eating. Whether alone or in the presence of others, take a breath and look at your plate before you begin eating. Chew mindfully and on purpose. Place your fork down between bites as you chew, and savor the flavor and textures of your food. Notice not only what you taste as you eat but also what you see and smell and how it sounds when you chew. Use all your God-given senses to practice eating presently and mindfully, showing gratitude for God's goodness with each bite.

closing prayer

Spirit,

Help me savor and appreciate the goodness you bring to the world around me. Please show me how to be salt and light.

Amen.

9
believe and breathe

Read reflectively: Luke 1:39-45

Blessed Among Women
Mary didn't waste a minute. She got up and traveled to a town in Judah in the hill country, straight to Zachariah's house, and greeted Elizabeth. When Elizabeth heard Mary's greeting, the baby in her womb leaped. She was filled with the Holy Spirit, and sang out exuberantly,

> You're so blessed among women,
>   and the babe in your womb, also blessed!
> And why am I so blessed that
>   the mother of my Lord visits me?

> The moment the sound of your
>   greeting entered my ears,
> The babe in my womb
>   skipped like a lamb for sheer joy.
> Blessed woman, who believed what God said,
>   believed every word would come true!

ponder this

Elizabeth displays joyous recognition and affirmation of Jesus' significance, even before his birth! Hearing Mary's greeting takes her breath away. She savors the gift of Mary's child within her family and is stunned by the reaction of the babe in her womb, John, who will be the announcer of Christ. She claims that the good things God has shown her will come to fruition—Mary's child and her own. May you believe and live into what God tells you to be good and true today.

guided meditation

Center yourself by breathing deeply or stretching your arms and legs. Then pause and imagine that your body is a musical instrument playing a wondrous song! Feel the sensation of your breath, in sync with the gentle rise and fall of your body as you breathe.

With each breath, imagine you are tuning your instrument, bringing it into perfect pitch.

Now, as you breathe deeply and slowly, focus on your heart. Notice your heart's gentle, rhythmic beating, like a soft and steady drumbeat. Can you feel your heartbeat without placing a hand on your body? Pause here as long as you need to, and notice your beating heart as you invite your breath to set the rhythm. Allow the breath and the heartbeat to become the foundation of your music, the steady rhythm that grounds you in God's goodness.

Take a moment to focus on your breath once more. Listen to the sound of your breath as it moves in and out.

Ponder the energy flowing in your body as an inner conductor guiding you now, breathing in sync with the imagined music God offers you.

Breathe steadily as this musical creation unfolds.

Ponder how your breath guides the music your body creates. What kind of music is it? Is your energy's tempo fast or slow today? Is it calming and peaceful like a lullaby, or is it upbeat and joyful like a lively dance? What rhythms and melodies does your breath imply?

Are you breathing in sync with your life song?

Say to yourself: *I breathe in God's goodness and welcome it in my life.*

Allow yourself to continue breathing in and receiving God's goodness as you return to the present moment.

soak in silence

Pause in the quiet and breathe purposefully. What do you sense?

for reflection

1. Do you believe God is near? Does your life feel in sync or out of sync with God?

2. Who or what takes your breath away or makes your heart skip a beat?

3. How might you live with more amazement and claim the good things around you?

sensory cue

Practice this simple breath exercise today, then return to it anytime you feel surprised, overwhelmed, out of sync, or disconnected and long to return to the present moment.

On your inhale, say to yourself: *I am breathing in.*
On your exhale, say to yourself: *I am breathing out.*
You can also add to this: *I am breathing in God's goodness. I am breathing out God's goodness.* This breath work practice encourages presence, helping you live more fully in the present, in the very life you have.

closing prayer

God,
Sync my breath with yours and help me live my life song.
Amen.

10
cleansed by God's touch

📖 Read reflectively: Luke 5:12-17

Invitation to a Changed Life
One day in one of the villages there was a man covered with leprosy. When he saw Jesus he fell down before him in prayer and said, "If you want to, you can cleanse me."

Jesus put out his hand, touched him, and said, "I want to. Be clean." Then and there his skin was smooth, the leprosy gone.

Jesus instructed him, "Don't talk about this all over town. Just quietly present your healed self to the priest, along with the offering ordered by Moses. Your cleansed and obedient life, not your words, will bear witness to what I have done." But the man couldn't keep it to himself, and the word got out. Soon a large crowd of people had gathered to listen and be healed of their sicknesses. As often as possible Jesus withdrew to out-of-the-way places for prayer.

One day as he was teaching, Pharisees and religion teachers were sitting around. They had come from nearly every village in Galilee and Judea, even as far away as Jerusalem, to be there. The healing power of God was on him.

ponder this

Jesus can indeed bring healing and restoration—physical and spiritual—to our lives. Jesus shows compassion and responds to a desperate plea for help from one who sought his healing touch. Jesus cleansed the man with his touch. Bring to mind one area of your life in which you long for God's healing touch as you enter this time of noticing.

guided meditation

With open hands upon your lap, center yourself with a breath. Now imagine yourself near a gently flowing mountain stream. The weather is ideal; you feel the perfect temperature on your skin. You choose to sit comfortably on a rock at the edge of the water and relax. You notice you have a companion in this space. God in human form, in the person of a man, Jesus, is seated beside you.

Jesus smiles at you and makes you feel welcome.

You sense something calming and restorative about the beautiful flowing water and the sounds you hear as the water passes. And now you know this is healing water. This water longs to remind you of the special properties it holds.

Jesus gazes at the stream and invites you to do the same. As you sit together, the water flows safely, taking your worries away.

You are curious about how simply being present with Jesus helps you feel such peace. Then you remember that Jesus is God in human form. He is there beside you, willing to hold your hand, meeting you in the flesh. The holy one you can always reach out to and touch. Like you, someone who has walked, talked, prayed, pondered, and been frustrated.

As you look at Jesus by the water's edge, you imagine your open hands reaching out to take his hand. It was there all along waiting for you, but you had not yet noticed it.

Upon touching Jesus, you feel stress and worry leave your body. As he holds your hand, you feel a calming sensation spread throughout your being. You are not alone beside this healing water. God is with you.

No words are needed; Jesus knows exactly how you need healing. He now pours the fresh healing water over your hands, and you feel changed.

Say to yourself: *I am cleansed by God, changed by Jesus' touch today.*

You feel restored and refreshed as you return to the present moment.

soak in silence

Pause in the quiet and breathe purposefully. What do you sense?

for reflection

1. Where do you need God's healing touch in your life today—physically, emotionally, spiritually?

2. Are you open to being cleansed by God? In what way?

3. How does the way you live your life reflect the healing God offers you? Does this change you?

sensory cue

When you need to calm yourself or find focus today, use this mindful exercise. Open your hands and gaze at your palms. Turn your attention to your fingers. Slowly start tapping your thumbs on one finger at a time, beginning with your pointer finger. Move across your fingers with the taps, working your way to your pinky finger, and then reverse directions to tap back to your pointer finger. Repeat as many times as you wish, remaining mindful and present with your own touch.

closing prayer

Creator-God,

I long to be cleansed and restored through your healing touch. I open my hands and welcome you now.

Amen.

Interlude
what does it mean to be whole?

Living a "With-God" Life

To live whole lives, we need to put to death thoughts that are not life-giving. When putting to death old ways and embracing life-giving alternatives, my most significant barrier is often myself. I hear internal messages that tear me down and take me away from God's wholeness. This is not God's voice, and it keeps me from living into the wholeness God offers.

Scripture tells us, "In Christ you have been brought to fullness" (Colossians 2:10, NIV).

Did you catch that? God has already completed us, brought us to fullness, and made us whole. The Creator has made us whole. Scripture teaches us that *because of Christ, we have everything we need within us to be whole and complete.* Take a deep breath and soak in that promise before you proceed.

This book is more than words on a page; it is an opportunity to use your whole self to connect with God. You are invited to release any limiting beliefs that are holding you back and to claim God's wholeness. What might you need to release to God today to do so?

As I write this book, my body faces several health challenges—none as significant as my stroke or brain surgery nearly twenty years ago, but enough to schedule some follow-ups with my physicians. As I age, I recognize now more than ever that life is fragile. Life is not to be taken for granted. When at one point I doubted my ability to truly *be* well, God helped me move past the barrier of myself (my doubts, my worries) and instead lean into a life *with God*—one that goes beyond what I can see or imagine and helps me be the whole person he created.

My spiritual director often reminds me of words I once said to her: my life is a "with-God" life.[1] I have moments and days when I forget this, but the deep longing in my heart is to live a "with-God" life every day, in every breath. *This* is living from a place of embodied presence no matter the storms, longing to live life to the fullest and not in the depths of despair. Especially when life is loud—full of stress, illness, busyness, and so on—we need to get quiet to connect with God and hear Jesus whisper, *Do you want to get well?*

Can you relate?

While you may not have anything physical holding you back from drawing close to God, there is undoubtedly some part of your life where you long to have God's healing touch. Ponder this for a moment, then consider:

- Do you believe you have already been made whole through Jesus?
- Do you think you can be well today?
- Who or what are you waiting for to fully immerse yourself in God's healing?

Living in wholeness looks different for everyone, but here's one thing I know for sure: You can say yes to the invitation to be whole before you understand *how* it may be possible. I did. You can too. Say yes to letting go of old patterns of unbelief and embrace your Creator's promise of wholeness.

11
show the way

Read reflectively: Mark 16:6-7

The Resurrection
[The angel at the tomb] said, "Don't be afraid. I know you're looking for Jesus the Nazarene, the One they nailed on the cross. He's been raised up; he's here no longer. You can see for yourselves that the place is empty. Now—on your way. Tell his disciples and Peter that he is going on ahead of you to Galilee. You'll see him there, exactly as he said."

ponder this

An angel explained that Jesus had been resurrected! This passage explores the reality of Jesus' resurrection, the role of his disciples as witnesses, and the assurance of his presence and guidance in days to come. It invites us to participate in gospel proclamation today by remembering the risen Christ's transformative power. Be open to God showing you the way as you enter this time of meditation.

guided meditation

Find a quiet, comfortable space to settle your body and center with your breath.

Imagine yourself standing at the edge of a long, deserted, tree-lined road. The sun begins to set, casting long shadows across the empty expanse before you. You are alone, and you recognize a sense of uncertainty in your heart.

As you step onto the road, notice how the ground feels beneath your feet. The seemingly endless road stretches out before you, and the silence is overwhelming. Your steps are slow and hesitant.

Now imagine Jesus appearing on this deserted road, covered in a gentle, warm light. He approaches you with a welcoming and comforting presence; notice him.

As he draws near, you feel a profound sense of peace and reassurance. His eyes are kind and understanding, and he extends his arms to you. You gaze upon his face and greet him.

As Jesus greets you, you feel the weight of your worries lifted from your heart. You are no longer alone on this journey. With Jesus by your side, you continue to walk down the deserted road, slow and steady yet companioned.

Envision the warmth of the light and Jesus' companionship as he walks with you, guiding your steps, showing you the way. Your pace becomes steadier, and your confidence grows. You can sense love, compassion, and wisdom emanating from his presence.

As you walk together, you may wish to share your worries, doubts, and fears with Jesus. He listens with a compassionate heart and provides guidance and comfort in return. Your troubles no longer burden you because you have a loving companion to share the road with.

Jesus pauses to offer you a gift. You gaze down and notice a box in his hands. As you open it, you are amazed by the gift you see inside. The gift Jesus offers is just what you need today. You feel awe and wonder. You are reassured that Jesus knows your every need and cares immensely for you. Pause with the gift you have been given and savor what it means to you.

You and Jesus continue walking, gift in hand. Imagine the road beginning to change. The path that was once deserted and desolate starts to transform.

With each step, you feel more peace, strength, and joy.

Say to yourself: *I journey with Jesus and the gifts he offers me.*

Take a moment to savor the sensation of walking with Jesus and seeing your gift. Allow this image to fill you with serenity and courage as you reenter your day.

soak in silence

Pause in the quiet and breathe purposefully. What do you sense?

for reflection

1. What gift did you see in the box, and what might that gift represent?

2. What does the gift of Christ's resurrection mean to you?

3. In what uncertain part of your life do you need Jesus to companion you and show you the way right now?

sensory cue

Practice hand yoga when you want to be reminded of God's presence and center yourself with purpose amid the unknowns of life. Allow your first finger (index finger) to touch the thumb gently, creating a circle while the other fingers remain extended. This is a common hand mudra (gesture) used in secular meditation and yoga practices; it is said to improve focus, concentration, and memory. Allow this simple gesture to help you center yourself with your Creator and remind you to be intentionally quiet with God as you choose to see Jesus at work in your life.

closing prayer

Jesus,

Please remind me you are near. Help me be open to receiving what you have for me today. And always show me the way, even when I am afraid.

Amen.

12
forgiveness and grace

Read reflectively: John 1:29-34

The God-Revealer
John saw Jesus coming toward him and yelled out, "Here he is, God's Passover Lamb! He forgives the sins of the world! This is the man I've been talking about, 'the One who comes after me but is really ahead of me.' I knew nothing about who he was—only this: that my task has been to get Israel ready to recognize him as the God-Revealer. That is why I came here baptizing with water, giving you a good bath and scrubbing sins from your life so you can get a fresh start with God."

John clinched his witness with this: "I watched the Spirit, like a dove flying down out of the sky, making himself at home in him. I repeat, I know nothing about him except this: The One who authorized me to baptize with water told me, 'The One on whom you see the Spirit

FORGIVENESS AND GRACE

come down and stay, this One will baptize with the Holy Spirit.' That's exactly what I saw happen, and I'm telling you, there's no question about it: *This* is the Son of God."

ponder this

This Scripture reminds us that Jesus, the Son of God, fulfills the messianic prophecies. It emphasizes Jesus' role as the ultimate sacrifice and Savior, bringing redemption, grace, and forgiveness to all who believe. John knew that Jesus was a gift for us, and we now know this too.

guided meditation

Settle in and take a moment to center yourself in your surroundings.

Now bring your attention to your breath. Feel the rise and fall of your chest and belly as you breathe in and out. Inhale deeply, filling your belly, and exhale slowly, releasing any tension, drawing your navel toward your spine.

Consider the powerful practice of self-forgiveness. It is natural for us to make mistakes and carry regrets, but forgiveness of oneself is a profound act of grace, self-compassion, and healing, which God already offers us.

Say to yourself: *I am forgiven.*

Now imagine standing under a waterfall of forgiveness. Hear the water rushing, sense the water covering your entire being—from your head to your toes. The water is welcome, the sounds are comforting, and you feel yourself being drenched not only by water but also by God's love, forgiveness, and grace.

Think of a time when you made a mistake or hurt yourself or someone else. Acknowledge the pain you may carry from that moment. Now imagine forgiving yourself for that time, for any regrets or self-blame. See yourself releasing the burden of guilt and negative self-judgment, allowing God's forgiving water to wash it away.

Allow Christ's grace to cover you, healing and nurturing your inner self. Because of what he has done, you are deserving of forgiveness.

Say to yourself: *I forgive myself.*

Feel the weight lifting off your shoulders, carried away by the divine. Forgiveness is a gift you can give to yourself, made possible by Christ, as it liberates you from the heavy burden of carrying past mistakes.

As the sound of the waterfall fades away, you realize God's love, forgiveness, and grace remain.

soak in silence

Pause in the quiet and breathe purposefully. What do you sense?

for reflection

1. What past mistakes do you release to God today?
2. How does it feel to forgive yourself or offer yourself grace?
3. Is there anything you need to hear from God to live more fully?

sensory cue

Recall these words to the hymn "Amazing Grace," written by John Newton:

> *Through many dangers, toils, and snares*
> *I have already come;*
> *'tis grace hath brought me safe thus far,*
> *and grace will lead me home.*[1]

Play or hum this hymn or another song today and welcome God's grace with your whole self. As you listen, breathe or sing with God. Consider moving your entire being as you sway or dance to the promise of this music, covered in God's forgiveness and grace.

closing prayer

Holy God,

Thank you for Jesus, who tells me how to live life each day—and covers me with forgiveness and grace.

Amen.

13

bittersweet moments

Read reflectively: Matthew 20:20-28

To Drink from the Cup

It was about that time that the mother of the Zebedee brothers came with her two sons and knelt before Jesus with a request.

"What do you want?" Jesus asked.

She said, "Give your word that these two sons of mine will be awarded the highest places of honor in your kingdom, one at your right hand, one at your left hand."

Jesus responded, "You have no idea what you're asking." And he said to James and John, "Are you capable of drinking the cup that I'm about to drink?"

They said, "Sure, why not?"

Jesus said, "Come to think of it, you *are* going to drink my cup. But as to awarding places of honor, that's not my business. My Father is taking care of that."

When the ten others heard about this, they lost their tempers, thoroughly disgusted with the two brothers. So Jesus got them together to settle things down. He said, "You've observed how godless rulers throw their weight around, how quickly a little power goes to their heads. It's not going to be that way with you. Whoever wants to be great must become a servant. Whoever wants to be first among you must be your slave. That is what the Son of Man has done: He came to serve, not be served—and then to give away his life in exchange for the many who are held hostage."

ponder this

This interaction occurs right after Jesus has described the events that will soon unfold—his approaching suffering, death, and resurrection—highlighting the purpose of his mission and the ultimate sacrifice he will make for humanity's redemption. It also reveals the disciples' misunderstanding and misplaced ambitions. Consider how bittersweet it must have been for Jesus to hold both truths. Consider how the reaction of the disciples surely impacted the story he was trying to tell with his life.

guided meditation

Recall from your memory one of your favorite dinner tables. You may have sat around this table as a child with your parents, or maybe now you sit around this table with your family or friends. Imagine a plate of fruit sitting before you. This fruit symbolizes both the bitter and the sweet moments of life. Reach out and take a piece of the fruit, feeling its texture.

As you bring the fruit closer to your nose, inhale its aroma. Does your jaw tense or relax?

Take a bite of the fruit and notice the taste on your tongue. Allow yourself to fully experience the flavors—bitter or sweet.

There may be a subtle sweetness that follows bitterness.

This fruit reflects life's complexity—the intermingling of joy and sorrow, happiness and pain.

As you continue to taste the fruit, reflect on your own life experiences—the moments around the table that have brought tears of sadness and happiness, the times of struggle that have led to growth, and the relationships that have left a mark on your heart. Pause and give God thanks for this fruit and those memories.

Allow these emotions to be present without judgment, knowing it is okay to feel a mix of emotions in response to life's bittersweet nature.

Say to yourself: *I am who I am today because of the bitter and the sweet.*

Pause and thank God for being with you along the way.

soak in silence

Pause in the quiet and breathe purposefully. What do you sense?

for reflection

1. What were the levels of feelings James and John may have felt in this passage?

2. What heedless words have come out of your mouth that you quickly regretted?

3. Recall a bittersweet moment from your life. Did you ever misunderstand something to later uncover more of the truth?

sensory cue

Bow your head. With humility, allow your eyes to fall toward your heart. Gaze on your heart with your eyes closed. Soften your eyes; release your jaw. Notice the softening in the back of the neck and upon the jawline. Exhale any remaining tensions out of your mouth with a sigh. Allow yourself to breathe in this bowed posture for several moments.

closing prayer

Father God,

Thank you for the gift of your Son, Jesus. Thank you for your companionship in all the moments of my life.

Amen.

14
shared life force

Read reflectively: Mark 2:13-17

The Tax Collector
Then Jesus went again to walk alongside the lake. Again a crowd came to him, and he taught them. Strolling along, he saw Levi, son of Alphaeus, at his work collecting taxes. Jesus said, "Come along with me." He came.

Later Jesus and his disciples were at home having supper with a collection of disreputable guests. Unlikely as it seems, more than a few of them had become followers. The religion scholars and Pharisees saw him keeping this kind of company and lit into his disciples: "What kind of example is this, acting cozy with the misfits?"

Jesus, overhearing, shot back, "Who needs a doctor: the healthy or the sick? I'm here inviting the sin-sick, not the spiritually-fit."

ponder this

Jesus' ministry is inclusive! He welcomes all people, not just some of them. We see Jesus' authority and power minister to the marginalized because God's radical invitation to discipleship is for all of us. May we respond to Jesus' inclusive ministry and extend love and acceptance to people from every walk of life.

guided meditation

Center in your space using your breath, extending the exhale as you relax your shoulders and jaw. Allow your gaze to soften down the tip of your nose after you read these words. Place one hand over your heart and feel the gentle beat. Now place your hand over your abdomen, noticing the breath move through your body as your belly expands and deflates. Your heartbeat and breath are reminders of your life force, and it's the same life force that connects you with all God's living beings. Take a moment to recognize this shared essence as you take a few breaths in and out of your nose with your hand upon your body.

Next, imagine yourself in a place with many people. It could be a busy city street, a sporting event, or even the grocery store. God's calming presence is upon you as you notice the different faces in your mind's eye in this place. Sense the shared connection you have with people who may appear different from you. Now, with each heartbeat and breath, you send waves of love, understanding, and care to each of these people, connecting you to them through the shared rhythm of life that God has gifted you.

Now extend this sense of connection and empathy beyond these faces, and bring to mind faces you know and love. Envision God's love connecting you with people from all walks of life—those who are merely faces in a crowd and those who are familiar to you.

Recognize that, like you, each of these individuals has lungs that breathe the same air as you and a heart that beats, experiences joy and pain, and seeks love and connection. With your next breath, offer as a prayer your heartfelt wishes for their well-being, happiness, and the gift of God's peace.

Say to yourself: *I am connected with all God's people. God gave us each a beating heart and the breath of life.*

Commit to carrying this sense of spiritual connection into your day. Remember the shared humanity that binds us together whenever you encounter someone—new or familiar. If you forget, place your hand on your heart and take a deep breath as a reminder.

soak in silence

Pause in the quiet and breathe purposefully. What do you sense?

for reflection

1. Who is an unlikely person you have befriended? What *do* you have in common?

2. Has your unlikely friendship or connection helped you grow as a person?

3. How has connecting with someone seemingly unlike you better helped you feel God's love?

sensory cue

Breathing through the nose (rather than the mouth) is quite beneficial to your entire being.[1] Practice breathing in and out of your nose today with these helpful steps. Close your mouth, then place a hand on your belly and a hand on your heart. Inhale slowly through your nose, allowing your belly to expand. At the top of your inhalation, slowly release the air out of your nose rather than your mouth. Practice nose breathing for several breaths at a time until this becomes more natural. If nose breathing is already natural for you, practice this breath work for five to ten minutes. Embrace this practice as you ponder the shared breath we all have access to.

closing prayer

Creator,

Help me offer your love and acceptance to another today. Thank you for our beating hearts and the breath of life.

Amen.

15
hand it over

Read reflectively: Matthew 9:18-26

Just a Touch
As [Jesus] finished [answering his disciples], a local official appeared, bowed politely, and said, "My daughter has just now died. If you come and touch her, she will live." Jesus got up and went with him, his disciples following along.

Just then a woman who had hemorrhaged for twelve years slipped in from behind and lightly touched his robe. She was thinking to herself, "If I can just put a finger on his robe, I'll get well." Jesus turned—caught her at it. Then he reassured her: "Courage, daughter. You took a risk of faith, and now you're well." The woman was well from then on.

By now they had arrived at the house of the town official, and pushed their way through the gossips looking for a story and the neighbors bringing in casseroles. Jesus was abrupt: "Clear out! This girl isn't dead. She's sleeping." They told him he didn't know what he was talking about. But when Jesus had gotten rid of the crowd, he went in, took the girl's hand, and pulled her to her feet—alive. The news was soon out, and traveled throughout the region.

ponder this

Jesus showed miraculous authority over sickness, disease, and even death. Think about Jesus' compassion and how he responded to the faith and desperation of those who sought miracles all those years ago. Hold space for his response to you as you seek miracles and invite him to touch your life today.

guided meditation

Begin by finding a comfortable position, either sitting or lying down. Take a few deep breaths, allowing yourself to relax as you seek refreshment and new life in God's presence today.

As you continue to breathe deeply, bring your awareness to your body. Visualize that you are drawing in fresh, revitalizing energy from God's Spirit with each inhalation. Imagine this energy as a vibrant, healing light entering your body, filling you with vitality and renewal.

Now shift your attention to any areas in your body where you feel tension or stagnant energy. It could be in your shoulders, neck, chest, abdomen, or elsewhere. Take a moment to identify one specific area in your body where you need God's touch.

As you focus on this one area, imagine gathering all the tension from that area of the body into a tight ball, making a fist. With your next breath, imagine squeezing that ball of stress tightly, holding it for a moment.

As you continue to breathe, feel the weight of that ball in your fist. What is it made of? Acknowledge that this stress and tension no longer serve you and are ready to be released.

Now, with a conscious intention, open your hand to God, letting go of that ball as you slowly release your grip. Imagine handing the ball of tension to Jesus, then visualize the tightness in your body dissipating into the air just as the ball is handed over, vanishing completely. Feel the weight lift off your body.

Take a moment to appreciate the sensation of lightness and spaciousness in this area of your body.

Feel the warmth and vibrancy of this fresh energy from God's touch.

Say to God: *I release what no longer serves me and savor the renewal that comes with your holy touch.*

Feel gratitude for Jesus' touch and for this opportunity to release and renew yourself in God's presence today.

soak in silence

Pause in the quiet and breathe purposefully. What do you sense?

for reflection

1. In which areas of your body do you long for a holy touch?
2. What is weighing you down today?
3. How do you feel about releasing the heaviness you carry to Jesus? Do you believe he can truly take it from you?

sensory cue

At some point in your day, shake off what is weighing you down. You may practice this seated or standing. Begin by shaking your hands, arms, feet, legs, core, hips, head, or other body parts for three to five breaths each, eventually shaking your entire body and releasing as you breathe. This activity may feel silly; allow yourself to laugh or giggle if those sensations arise. Place your hands on your body, and notice how your body feels after your shaking exercise.

closing prayer

Holy One,

Refresh me with your touch and help me release to you what does not serve me today.

Amen.

Interlude
savoring the Scriptures
The Practice of Lectio Divina

If you are not familiar with lectio divina, allow me to introduce you to a profound way of reading and meditating on Scripture that has been used for centuries in monastic communities. *Lectio divina* is Latin for "sacred reading." It treats Scripture as the living Word, not simply a text to be read. Put another way: The goal of this time is to read for formation, not for information.

There are four steps to the process: *read, reflect, respond,* and *rest*. Shall we try this together?

We'll be using John 5:1-6 as the Scripture for this practice. You are invited to read the Scripture slowly three times in the style of lectio divina. You may read it silently, read it aloud, or even listen to an audio version of this passage. However you choose to read it, truly hear the words Jesus spoke as if they are being spoken aloud today.

Prepare yourself for this practice by inviting God to speak to you through this particular Scripture passage.

> Soon another Feast came around and Jesus was back in Jerusalem. Near the Sheep Gate in Jerusalem there was a pool, in Hebrew called *Bethesda*, with five alcoves. Hundreds of sick people—blind, crippled,

paralyzed—were in these alcoves. One man had been an invalid there for thirty-eight years. When Jesus saw him stretched out by the pool and knew how long he had been there, he said, "Do you want to get well?"
JOHN 5:1-6

Then follow these instructions from *Holy Listening with Breath, Body, and the Spirit*:

1. **LECTIO/READ.** Read or listen to the designated passage once slowly.

2. **MEDITATIO/REFLECT.** Read or listen to the passage again. Consider a word, phrase, or image from the passage that draws your attention. What stands out to you? What do you hear, see, or sense? Reflect on how this word, image, or phrase speaks to you today. If it's a word or a phrase, consider repeating it silently to yourself.

3. **ORATIO/RESPOND.** Read or listen to the passage again. Respond to what you hear in God's Word and how it makes you feel. Is there an invitation for you—for your breath, body, or spirit—in the Scripture passage today? Tell God what you heard or sensed.

4. **CONTEMPLATIO/REST.** Rest in what you have heard. Receive any clarity, stillness, insight, or imagery that comes to your mind. Give God thanks for this time, and rest in the Word of God.[1]

Do you want to get well? As you sit with this passage and with Jesus, consider what this Scripture may be inviting you into today. You can use these instructions for any of the passages in this book or in the Bible. Savor the words as you explore what God may be inviting you to notice.

16
encountering Christ

Read reflectively: Luke 24:13-16

> *The Road to Emmaus*
> That same day two of [the disciples] were walking to the village Emmaus, about seven miles out of Jerusalem. They were deep in conversation, going over all these things that had happened. In the middle of their talk and questions, Jesus came up and walked along with them. But they were not able to recognize who he was.

ponder this

The disciples' encounter with the risen Jesus validates their experience of doubt, confusion, and lack of recognition before coming to a revelation of his identity. This story highlights the journey of faith and the importance of recognizing Jesus' presence with us always. In our everyday lives, we, too, are capable of encountering the resurrected Christ and experiencing the transformative power that comes with his presence—if we are willing to pause and notice that he is near.

guided meditation

Scan your body from head to toe, noticing any tension or tightness. Breathe into those areas and let them soften and release. Relax your body into your seat with each breath. Invite God to come close to you in this time of quiet reflection so that you may recognize and feel the presence of Christ with you now.

Turn your attention inward and invite any emotions present to arise before God. You may see sadness, happiness, grief, gratitude, or even rage. Pause for a moment to be present with these or others.

Now that you see your emotions more clearly, take a moment to name them before your Creator today.

Welcome them without judgment. What emotions are present for you? What emotions may be buried or hidden within you? Are there any emotions you prefer to squelch or ignore?

Observe how these emotions feel in your body. Now ask God, *If my emotions were a color, what color would they be?* Ask God to help you see your emotions clearly and create a true, vivid picture of what arises within you.

Try not to change what you are seeing or feeling. Instead, let your emotions arise naturally and share them honestly with God. Allow your Creator to be near you in all that you are sensing today.

Pray: *Be with me as I claim my many emotions.*

Take a moment to reflect on the emotions you noticed during this time of reflection. Be kind to yourself and ask God to help you receive any wisdom or insight available from the feelings you are carrying.

soak in silence

Pause in the quiet and breathe purposefully. What do you sense?

for reflection

1. Were you surprised by any emotions, feelings, or colors that arose in the quiet?
2. Are there emotions within you that you prefer to avoid noticing?
3. In what circumstance is Jesus walking with you right now?

sensory cue

Consider journaling through, drawing, or listing the emotions within you today to visualize what God is companioning you in now. If you envisioned your emotions as having a color, find a marker or crayon and write the name of each emotion in the color you saw or sensed. Place your list of emotions in a place that is important to you.

closing prayer

God,
Help me see and recognize you in my life and in my feelings. I want to encounter you in all I face and never miss your presence.
Amen.

17
inner clarity

Read reflectively: Matthew 5:8

You're Blessed
[Jesus said,] "You're blessed when you get your inside world—your mind and heart—put right. Then you can see God in the outside world."

ponder this

Jesus extends an invitation to seek inner clarity, indicating that when your inner world (including your thoughts and emotions) is aligned with God's principles, you can better perceive God's presence and work in the external world. This passage encourages us to focus on inner spiritual transformation to better understand the divine in our lives. As you settle into this time, be reminded that it is not always about what we see with our eyes but also what we hear within our spirits.

guided meditation

Allow your hands to rest in your lap, take a deep breath, and ask God to help you listen for your longings and desires. Then ask yourself, *What do I long for?* Pause here as you wait for your reply.

As you breathe deeply, notice what comes forth, and accept it without judgment. Be reminded that the thoughts and emotions we have are a natural part of our inner landscape and how God made us. Ask the Holy Spirit to help you release any outside expectations and connect with your own intuition.

Ask yourself again, *What do I long for?* Pause and listen.

Now imagine a clear pool of water. This pool represents your inner clarity. It may have many ripples or waves to start. With each breath, visualize your pool becoming stiller, calmer, and clearer. It may take time; be patient. As the pool calms, with God's help, you will reach a place where there will be no ripples, no sounds to distract you, and you can hear the truth come through.

Say to yourself: *With God's help, I will keep listening for my longings and the truth.*

Be still. Notice the quiet settle over the water. Feel the stillness settle over your body. Allow this quiet stillness to envelop you.

Express gratitude for the opportunity to explore your inner world with the one who created you. Thank God for a moment of quiet calm and for the Holy Spirit's help to seek inner clarity.

soak in silence

Pause in the quiet and breathe purposefully. What do you sense?

for reflection

1. Does being quiet with God come easily for you, or is it challenging?
2. Do culture and commercialism push you into expectations that do not align with your true longings?
3. Are there areas of your inner life that do not match your outer life?

sensory cue

Step outside today for a time of walking meditation. Whether you walk in a quiet neighborhood or a loud city, be reminded that God is with you. With each step, be mindful of the sensations around you. Isolate each sense. First, notice what you hear, then what you see, then what you smell, then what you taste. Finally, pick up something you can touch. What do you notice in your body as you isolate each sense? Do you gain inner clarity? Be present in the world, open your heart to gratitude, and walk slowly and mindfully, allowing yourself to experience the presence of God and God's Kingdom in and around you. As you walk, remember that your Creator guides you through what you hear, see, and sense—inside and out.

closing prayer

God,

Thank you for helping me pause and listen. Now may I listen for you and notice you more clearly within and in the world around me.

Amen.

18
partake in the blessings

📖 Read reflectively: Mark 14:22-25

"This Is My Body"
In the course of their meal, having taken and blessed the bread, [Jesus] broke it and gave it to [the disciples]. Then he said,

> Take, this is my body.

Taking the chalice, he gave it to them, thanking God, and they all drank from it. He said,

> This is my blood,
> God's new covenant,
> Poured out for many people.

"I'll not be drinking wine again until the new day when I drink it in the kingdom of God."

ponder this

The Lord's Supper is a symbol of Jesus' sacrifice for us. It emphasizes the redemptive significance of Jesus' body and blood, inviting believers to participate in this remembrance and partake in the spiritual blessings of God's promises for us. Pause for a moment and give thanks for the sacrifices Christ made for you and for all humankind.

guided meditation

Travel in your mind to biblical times and imagine you are present when Christ shares the bread and the cup with his disciples. See yourself sitting at the table with the disciples. You may find yourself unclear about the significance of this gathering, like the disciples. Yet, in the presence of Jesus, you are drawn to partake in the bread and cup set before you simply because it was set by him.

Take a deep breath and momentarily let go of any questions or doubts. Turn your attention to the elements on the table. Before you is a piece of bread and a cup of wine.

Start by noticing the piece of bread, feeling its weight and texture in your hand. Let your fingers trace the contours of the bread's surface, exploring its roughness and warmth. This bread is more than just sustenance; it represents the body of Christ, broken for you. Take a moment to reflect on the sacrifice and love behind this act.

Now bring the bread to your lips but wait to take your imagined bite. Feel the anticipation and wonder as you prepare to partake in this sacred meal. As you raise the bread to your mouth, take a moment to inhale deeply and savor the aroma.

When you're ready, mindfully take a bite of the bread. Pay close attention to the taste, the texture, and the flavors that flood your senses. Notice how the bread crumbles, how the grains taste, and whether your mouth is moist or dry. This simple act of eating becomes a profound connection to Christ's teachings. What does this experience taste like?

As you chew, let your mind and heart reflect on moments of guidance and compassion from Jesus that have touched your soul. Allow this bread to nourish not only your body but also your spirit.

Now take an imagined sip from the cup of wine, feeling its smooth surface against your lips. As the wine flows into your mouth, savor the warmth it brings. Swallow intentionally. This cup of grapes represents Christ's blood, shed for the forgiveness of sins and the promise of eternal life. What does this experience taste like?

Pray: *Thank you for your presence and promises through the bread and the cup.*

As you continue to imagine yourself as part of this passage, let the promises of God fill more than your tastebuds—also your thoughts and your heart. Relish the gift of this sacred meal, allowing it to deepen your understanding and strengthen your connection to Christ.

soak in silence

Pause in the quiet and breathe purposefully. What do you sense?

for reflection

1. What does it feel like to use your imagination to enter Scripture and partake in Communion?

2. How do you think the disciples felt when Jesus offered them the bread and the cup?

3. How might you have reacted if you had been sitting at the table and did not know the rest of the story, as you do today?

sensory cue

For your next Communion experience, recall this meditation and practice being in the moment with Jesus, mindfully smelling, tasting, and touching the elements that serve as symbols of God's promises.

closing prayer

Jesus,
Let me taste your presence and promises.
Amen.

19

wondrous love

📖 Read reflectively: John 12:1-3

Anointing His Feet

Six days before Passover, Jesus entered Bethany where Lazarus, so recently raised from the dead, was living. Lazarus and his sisters invited Jesus to dinner at their home. Martha served. Lazarus was one of those sitting at the table with them. Mary came in with a jar of very expensive aromatic oils, anointed and massaged Jesus' feet, and then wiped them with her hair. The fragrance of the oils filled the house.

ponder this

Mary's single-minded focus on expressing her love for Jesus is highlighted in this passage. It underscores the importance of genuine and selfless devotion to Jesus, which involves giving one's best without reservation. Mary shows us what it looks like to not worry about the world and instead draw close to our Creator, no matter the cost.

guided meditation

Imagine yourself lying down on your back with your arms spread wide, palms facing up, relaxed and open. You are in an open field under a clear, infinite sky.

Start by taking a few deep breaths. Feel the rhythm of your breath as it flows in and out naturally. Imagine breathing in the fragrance of the oils that Mary used in today's Scripture passage. Allow the scent to calm your mind and your spirit.

Visualize Jesus gently anointing your feet with oil. Pause to appreciate his tender touch. Feel God's love and grace flow into your being. Release your self into the earth beneath you.

As you rest in God's love, release any burdens, worries, or doubts you may be carrying. Surrender them to Jesus' love.

Take a moment to bask in the warmth and love that surround you. God's presence fills every cell of your body, bringing peace, comfort, and healing.

Say to yourself: *I am loved by God.*

As you go about your day, breathe in the love and peace you have experienced so you can share God's love with others.

soak in silence

Pause in the quiet and breathe purposefully. What do you sense?

for reflection

1. Can you recall a time when someone showed you extravagant love? What was that experience like for you?
2. Can you recall a time when you showed extravagant love? How did that feel?
3. How might you offer Jesus a sign of your extravagant love today?

sensory cue

Ponder a scent that reminds you of God's love. From holy incense to garden flowers to freshly baked cookies, many scents may come to mind. Different smells can trigger our amazing brains to recall memories and sensations related to these smells. These smells can help us feel connected to our memories more deeply. If possible, seek out a scent you recall and experience it today. Inhale the real or imagined aroma and sense what it feels like to be loved by God.

closing prayer

Holy One,
Thank you for the abundant love you pour on me. May I never take it for granted.
Amen.

20
new life

📖 Read reflectively: Luke 2:8-14

An Event for Everyone
There were shepherds camping in the neighborhood. They had set night watches over their sheep. Suddenly, God's angel stood among them and God's glory blazed around them. They were terrified. The angel said, "Don't be afraid. I'm here to announce a great and joyful event that is meant for everybody, worldwide: A Savior has just been born in David's town, a Savior who is Messiah and Master. This is what you're to look for: a baby wrapped in a blanket and lying in a manger."

At once the angel was joined by a huge angelic choir singing God's praises:

> Glory to God in the heavenly heights,
> Peace to all men and women on earth who please him.

ponder this

An angel announces the birth of Jesus and proclaims peace and joy for all people. This news emphasizes the transformative impact of Jesus' birth. It invites us to respond with awe, joy, wonder, and praise. May we now recognize the significance of Jesus as the Savior who brings reconciliation and peace.

guided meditation

Center yourself and settle into your space by breathing deeply. Now bring to mind the image of a sleeping newborn baby. Picture the baby's tiny fingers and toes. Visualize the soft, rhythmic rise and fall of the chest as the baby breathes, a reminder of the miracle of life. Match your breath to the baby's; pause here as long as you wish to breathe in this way.

Reflect on the profound wonder that healthy newborns bring into our lives. They arrive anew, seemingly untouched by the world. Consider the transformation that newborns bring. Imagine how they unite families and remind us of the simple joys in life. Newborns are often a symbol of hope and new beginnings.

Now imagine yourself holding this newborn in your arms. Feel the warmth and softness against your skin and smell the newness. As you cradle the baby, you feel a deep connection and sense of love. This unconditional love reflects the boundless capacity for God's love within you.

Ponder for a moment the endless possibilities that arise with new beginnings. Just as newborns bring new hope, they also invite you to embrace change and growth in your own life. They inspire you to see the beauty in the ordinary, embrace miracles, and welcome transformation.

As we close this time of reflection, take with you the sense of wonder, love, and hope that a newborn baby brings. Carry this with you as you go about your day, and remember that each day is an opportunity for a new beginning with Christ.

soak in silence

Pause in the quiet and breathe purposefully. What do you sense?

for reflection

1. How are you reaching for hope or a new beginning?
2. How might Christ meet you in this yearning?
3. Who might accompany you along the way?

sensory cue

Many emotions beyond hope are connected to the birth of a newborn. Some new parents experience fear or worry, just as the shepherds did in this passage. The sensory cue of touch can help ground your memories and provide a tangible connection to the emotions and imagery in this meditation.

Find a soft, textured item to hold. It could be a plush toy, a soft blanket, a piece of fabric, a feather, a baby doll, or anything that feels gentle and comforting. As you hold your item, feel its softness, texture, and warmth. Imagine it as a symbol of a newborn baby's soft skin and warmth; allow your touch sensation to draw you close to the baby sent for us, Christ, and be reminded of the new life within you.

closing prayer

Jesus,
Awaken hope in me even when I feel afraid.
Amen.

Interlude
connecting with God

Living like the Christian Mystics

We are made exactly as God wants us to be.
We only need to lift our minds above Earth's empty
sorrows so that we can rejoice in the Divine joy.
JULIAN OF NORWICH (CA. 1342–CA. 1416)

When I began my seminary journey, my first class was on the Christian mystics. I had no idea what to expect, and after some initial shock (books written hundreds or even thousands of years ago can be challenging to read), I was pleasantly surprised.

This class was taught in an intensive format where our in-person hours were long and focused on the writings of the Christian mystics. My body was living in chronic pain at the time. Sitting for long periods caused my body intense pain and often took away from my ability to be mindful and present.

When my professor announced she would be reading from the mystics for hours on our first afternoon together, I panicked. It may have been the look on my face, but quickly she offered us the chance to move or shift as we listened to her read. She even offered a yoga mat, and I took advantage of that opportunity. She knew it caused me pain to sit for long periods, making it hard to listen. Gentle movement helped.

In those hours, I shifted from chair to mat, from sitting to standing, and I organically moved and breathed and listened as the mystic words poured over me. As our professor read aloud to us, without any pain arising in my body, I soaked in these words, which were like nothing I had ever heard. My soul came alive when I included my body in listening to the wisdom of these saints. Have you ever had an experience that was deepened because you invited your body into the listening experience? If not, consider this book an opportunity to do just that.

Evelyn Underhill, a Christian writer who lived from 1875 until 1941, explained mysticism as "an overwhelming consciousness of God and of [one's] own soul."[1] She reminded us that connecting with God invites an awareness we cannot find by accident. We can live like mystics today, however, if we are willing to pause and welcome God into our everyday moments.

The Christian mystics offer much regarding embodied living through their ancient writings. They can help us understand the integration of the physical and spiritual dimensions of human existence. While their beliefs and backgrounds vary, there are common characteristics among the mystics that help us on our embodied-living journeys.

Here is some of what the mystics have taught me over the years and how they may help your own body and soul care as you enter these sensory meditations of presence:

- **UNION WITH GOD IN THE PRESENT MOMENT:** The mystics teach that connecting with the divine is not some far-off, unattainable goal. Instead, they help us understand that we can encounter God in the ordinary experiences of life. This reminds us to be fully present, aware, and engaged in everyday experiences.

- **EMBODIED LIVING:** The mystics teach about caring for the physical body through lifestyle choices and recognizing the interconnectedness of human existence. All they say and do reflect a "with-God" life.

- **CONTEMPLATIVE PRACTICES:** The mystics value silence, prayer, and meditation as vital aspects to deepen one's connection with their Creator. These are not simply quiet, intellectual experiences but whole-body practices to engage oneself and connect with God's Spirit.

- **LOVE:** A common theme among many of the writings of the mystics is love. Let us embrace love for our Creator, love for one another, love for God's creation, and love for ourselves to live as the mystics lived.

If you remember nothing else, I invite you to carry this final point about love with you as you move forward. God's love is shared through Jesus in each of the Gospels. If you long for God's healing and wholeness, you must prioritize God's loving presence.

21
looking to understand

Read reflectively: Luke 18:31-34

I Want to See Again
Then Jesus took the Twelve off to the side and said, "Listen carefully. We're on our way up to Jerusalem. Everything written in the Prophets about the Son of Man will take place. He will be handed over to the Romans, jeered at, ridiculed, and spit on. Then, after giving him the third degree, they will kill him. In three days he will rise, alive." But they didn't get it, could make neither heads nor tails of what he was talking about.

ponder this

When Jesus predicted his death and resurrection, the disciples did not understand. Today's passage reveals Jesus' foreknowledge of the events in Jerusalem and the disciples' inability to grasp the significance of these words. This theme challenges us to seek deeper understanding of Jesus' teachings and to trust in God's divine wisdom and purpose, even when we cannot see or understand.

guided meditation

Take a few centering breaths, then welcome this simple eye-movement meditation to center, ground, and become more aware of all Jesus is helping you see in your life today. You may wish to read the instructions and then follow your instincts to practice this meditation in a way that feels right for you.

> **BEGIN BY LOOKING UP:** With your eyes open or closed, gently lift your gaze upward, looking up to welcome Christ's presence. Hold this gaze for a few seconds.
>
> **LOOK DOWN:** Now slowly lower your gaze, looking downward within yourself. Hold this gaze for a few seconds.
>
> **LOOK TO THE LEFT:** Shift your gaze to the left, symbolizing your willingness to explore new horizons. Hold this gaze for a few seconds.
>
> **LOOK TO THE RIGHT:** Now turn your gaze to the right, representing your receptivity to the world's beauty and wonder. Hold this gaze for a few seconds.
>
> **BACK TO CENTER:** Return your gaze to the center, reminding yourself that Christ is the center of your life and that you long to have your eyes always focused on God.

Pray: *Jesus, help me keep my eyes on you.*

LOOKING TO UNDERSTAND

soak in silence

Pause in the quiet and breathe purposefully. What do you sense?

for reflection

1. Has there ever been a time when you did not understand your life direction or it was unclear to you? How did you look to Jesus during that time?
2. Who helps guide your spiritual path?
3. What are some ways you can keep your eyes on Jesus?

sensory cue

Light a candle (traditional wax or battery operated), preferably in a dim room, and place it at eye level before you. Take a few deep breaths and choose to set aside distractions for at least one minute. Allow your eyes to focus softly on the light of the flame and follow its movements, blinking as little as possible. Observe what you notice or feel after your time of candle gazing.

closing prayer

Lord,
Help me look for you even when I cannot see or understand all the details.
Amen.

22

love others

Read reflectively: Mark 12:28-31

The Most Important Commandment
One of the religion scholars came up. Hearing the lively exchanges of question and answer and seeing how sharp Jesus was in his answers, he put in his question: "Which is most important of all the commandments?"

Jesus said, "The first in importance is, 'Listen, Israel: The Lord your God is one; so love the Lord God with all your passion and prayer and intelligence and energy.' And here is the second: 'Love others as well as you love yourself.' There is no other commandment that ranks with these."

ponder this

Jesus challenges us to examine our own lives and attitudes, urging us to prioritize our love for God above all else and to express that love through our actions toward and relationships with others. He calls for a selfless and sacrificial love that mirrors the love of God. Pause and listen for God's loving-kindness as you enter this time of reflection.

guided meditation

Find a comfortable posture in which to meditate on God's love for you and for others today. Once you feel settled into the quiet, repeat silently or aloud:

> *May I be filled with God's love.*
> *May I be happy.*
> *May I be healthy.*
> *May I be at peace.*

Now ask the Holy Spirit to bring a loved one to mind. Listen for the name of someone you care deeply about—a family member or friend. Visualize their face in your mind. Say silently or aloud:

> *May* _____ [name] *be filled with God's love. May* _____ [name] *be happy. May* _____ [name] *be healthy. May* _____ [name] *be at peace.*

Gradually widen your circle of compassion. Listen for the name of an acquaintance, neighbor, or coworker. Visualize that person's face and repeat silently or aloud:

> *May* _____ [name] *be filled with God's love. May* _____ [name] *be happy. May* _____ [name] *be healthy. May* _____ [name] *be at peace.*

Now broaden your focus to include all living beings. Imagine the whole world hearing your prayer today.

Say: *May all beings be filled with God's love. May all beings be happy. May all beings be healthy. May all beings be at peace.*

As invited by Jesus, allow God's love to be freely shared through this time of meditation. Imagine God's love touching every corner of the earth, bringing love, healing, and the unity of Christ as you close this loving-kindness meditation.

soak in silence

Pause in the quiet and breathe purposefully. What do you sense?

for reflection

1. Who has shared God's love with you recently? How did you respond?

2. How does it feel in your body when you do something for someone else simply out of love, without the goal of receiving anything in return?

3. Listen for God to bring someone to mind today that you could offer loving-kindness to beyond this prayer time.

sensory cue

Ask the Holy Spirit to whisper ways you can offer acts of kindness today without the goal of recognition or reward. Be listening throughout your day for ways the Spirit is prompting you. Engage in an act of service, provide comfort to someone who is hurting, or give back in another way to tangibly express God's love. If not today, discern the right time, and follow through on serving another with God's love.

closing prayer

Lord,

Help me listen to your promptings and commit daily to loving others as you love.

Amen.

23
fed by God

† Read reflectively: John 6:1-6

Bread and Fish for All
Jesus went across the Sea of Galilee (some call it Tiberias). A huge crowd followed him, attracted by the miracles they had seen him do among the sick. When he got to the other side, he climbed a hill and sat down, surrounded by his disciples. It was nearly time for the Feast of Passover, kept annually by the Jews.

When Jesus looked out and saw that a large crowd had arrived, he said to Philip, "Where can we buy bread to feed these people?" He said this to stretch Philip's faith. He already knew what he was going to do.

ponder this

Jesus' ability to transcend human limitations and provide abundantly for people's needs reminds us that he is God's Son. Jesus has compassion for the physical needs of those who follow him, and he has the power to work miracles to meet those needs. As you enter this time of reflection, allow yourself to be fed by God today.

guided meditation

Pause and imagine you are in a bountiful garden. Picture the vibrant colors, the lush greenery, and the fragrant blossoms surrounding you. Feel the sun's warmth on your skin and the gentle breeze in the air.

As you explore this beautiful garden, notice the bounty of vegetables surrounding you. They are ripe, vibrant, and inviting. Take a moment to appreciate the variety and richness of this garden, a symbol of the abundance that life has to offer you.

Now, in this garden, you hear a soft, loving voice. Jesus invites you to taste any or all of the vegetables that capture your attention. The presence of Christ is warm and comforting.

Choose a vegetable that draws you in. It may be something you have never tried or a favorite that brings back fond memories. Reach out, pluck it from the branch or vine, and hold it.

Feel the texture, smell the aroma, and appreciate the gift before you, lingering as you do so. As you take a bite, savor the flavors that burst in your mouth. What does the vegetable taste like? Let the taste be a reminder of the richness of life.

As you continue to explore this plentiful garden, feel free to try more vegetables. Each one is a unique experience, a blessing to be enjoyed. Allow yourself to be present in the moment, fully immersed in the abundance.

As you savor the blessings, remember that life, like a bountiful garden, is full of abundance and grace. Say to yourself: *I welcome God's blessings.*

Carry the sense of abundance and blessings with you as you continue your day. Know that you are connected to the source of infinite love and abundance, your Creator.

soak in silence

Pause in the quiet and breathe purposefully. What do you sense?

for reflection

1. Which blessings from God have surprised you?
2. When have you experienced God's bounty?
3. How might you thank God for the bountiful blessings bestowed upon you?

sensory cue

Handwrite a list of your blessings today. Then speak those blessings aloud, reviewing your list with gratitude and appreciation for the abundance in your life.

closing prayer

Lord,
Help me recognize the ways you care for me and bless me each day. May I not take my blessings for granted.
Amen.

24
prophetic presence

Read reflectively: Luke 4:16-21

To Set the Burdened Free
He came to Nazareth where he had been raised. As he always did on the Sabbath, he went to the meeting place. When he stood up to read, he was handed the scroll of the prophet Isaiah. Unrolling the scroll, he found the place where it was written,

> God's Spirit is on me;
> > he's chosen me to preach the Message of good news
> > > to the poor,
> Sent me to announce pardon to prisoners and
> > recovery of sight to the blind,
> To set the burdened and battered free,
> > to announce, "This is God's time to shine!"

He rolled up the scroll, handed it back to the assistant, and sat down. Every eye in the place was on him, intent. Then he started in, "You've just heard Scripture make history. It came true just now in this place."

ponder this

This passage sets the tone for Jesus' ministry. It reveals his authority and the significance of his role as the promised Messiah, bringing hope and liberation to the world. Jesus lived and breathed on this very earth, fulfilling God's promises. He clearly understood his purpose and that it aligned with the prophetic words spoken from Scripture.

guided meditation

Find a quiet and comfortable place to sit with a tall, long spine. Now reach your head high and straighten your posture. Read these words, then soften or close your eyes and take a deep breath in. As you exhale, welcome Christ's presence now.

Begin by pondering the image of the prophetic Christ. See him standing and breathing on this very earth. Consider that the word *breath* in Scripture is used interchangeably with the word *spirit*.[1] As you breathe, welcome God's Spirit to fill you completely.

Now imagine that Jesus is standing beside you. He is fully present with you, filled with breath and life. He is rooted and grounded not only in God but also on the physical earth—he is standing tall and confident.

As you continue to breathe deeply and slowly, visualize and imagine the confidence that Christ is rooted in rising up from the earth and into the soles of your feet, rooting and connecting you to the earth and to God. Allow this rootedness to travel all the way to the top of your head. Welcome this grounded sensation to fill your entire being. Sit up tall as you breathe.

Say to yourself, *I breathe and receive Jesus' prophetic presence today.* Continue to breathe deeply and slowly, basking in the strong and comforting presence of Christ. Carry this groundedness into your day as you take three closing breaths.

soak in silence

Pause in the quiet and breathe purposefully. What do you sense?

for reflection

1. Consider that Jesus breathed this earth's air like you do today. How does that make you feel?
2. Did you remember that Jesus fulfills this prophecy as spoken from the book of Isaiah?
3. Can you begin to comprehend God's purpose in your own life?

sensory cue

Either now or before you go to bed tonight, practice this abbreviated version of progressive muscle relaxation to help release tension and stress from your body. Studies show that this simple technique has many benefits for your body and mind.[2] After a full breath in and a long, extended exhale out, begin by tensing all the muscles in your face and scalp. Do not strain, but create enough tension so that you can feel when you relax. Squinch your entire face, closing your eyes, nose, and mouth as tightly as possible, and move your ears up if you are able. Hold this for a count of five to eight as you inhale. Now relax completely. Soften every part of your face and head as you breathe into the release and this relaxed sensation.

You may stop here or gradually tighten and relax other muscle groups in your body. If you continue, move on to your shoulders and chest, then your core and hips, all the way down to your legs and feet.

Notice any sensations you feel within your own body and be amazed at the responsiveness of your physical being.

closing prayer

Lord,

Help me breathe in your Spirit and sense your prophetic presence in and around me today.

Amen.

25

held and changed

Read reflectively: Luke 5:17-20

Invitation to a Changed Life
One day as [Jesus] was teaching, Pharisees and religion teachers were sitting around. They had come from nearly every village in Galilee and Judea, even as far away as Jerusalem, to be there. The healing power of God was on him.

Some men arrived carrying a paraplegic on a stretcher. They were looking for a way to get into the house and set him before Jesus. When they couldn't find a way in because of the crowd, they went up on the roof, removed some tiles, and let him down in the middle of everyone, right in front of Jesus. Impressed by their bold belief, he said, "Friend, I forgive your sins."

ponder this

Jesus' response offers healing and a changed life for the paralytic man and his friends. In this story, Jesus is addressing not only the physical ailment the man is experiencing but also his spiritual well-being. Ponder the commitment of this man's friends to physically set him before God. Consider how their actions invited the man to be healed and to live a changed life.

guided meditation

Imagine you are resting securely in a lush hammock supported by two strong and rooted trees. Your entire body is being held, safely cocooned, by the hammock. As you inhale, breathe into the front, back, and sides of your body. Allow your entire core to expand and take up space—inviting the imagined hammock to expand on this breath in. As you exhale, allow your entire core to deflate as you settle and rest in the imagined hammock. The Holy Spirit is with you as the hammock holds you and the trees support the weight of your body.

Soften your body into the hammock, and let go of any worries, guilt, or regrets you may carry. With each breath, feel held by the care of the hammock instead. Notice how it feels in your body or spirit to be held in this way, with no effort or work on your part. Envision the hammock and its trees supporting you as you relax. As you breathe deeply, surrender entirely to the Holy Spirit. Feel the safety that surrounds you. Let go of any need to control, fix, or change anything. Allow yourself to simply be held before God, resting in the Spirit's presence now.

Pray: *I am changed by being in your presence.*

When you are ready to return to your day, do so slowly, carrying with you the sense of being held securely, with love and care.

soak in silence

Pause in the quiet and breathe purposefully. What do you sense?

for reflection

1. Think of a time when someone has held or cared for you.
2. Think of a time when you have held or cared for a friend or other loved one.
3. How might your life change if you allowed others to support you more often in your journey toward Jesus?

sensory cue

Hold your hands out before you. Look closely at your hands with palms up and then with palms down. As you gaze, notice any scars or wrinkles. Your hands have been through a lot. They have cared, and they have been cared for. Your hands connect you to others, they open to receive, and they even clench in resistance. Your hands have held and been held. Your hands have changed over time. Bring your hands to your heart with palms together to symbolize a prayer posture, and give thanks for your hands.

closing prayer

Jesus,

Help me seek support when I need it from those who accompany me on this spiritual journey. Show me how to be spiritual support for others along the way too.

Amen.

Interlude
embracing the gift of rest
A Countercultural Call

In *This Here Flesh*, Cole Arthur Riley brings each page to life with stories of embodied presence as she shares about the generational trauma she has to actively work to escape due to the enslavement of her ancestors. She talks about a God who is here in her present life and reminds us of the importance of going slow in a world that makes that nearly impossible.

Is there something in your past or present that you are working to escape from? If so, this likely shows up in your body and your day-to-day actions. Riley says, "We have found ourselves too busy for beauty. We spin our bodies into chaos with the habits and expectations of the dominating culture, giving and doing and working."[1] We must not be too busy for beauty within and around us. We need to find permission to go slow even when it is ingrained in us to move fast, or when it is nearly impossible due to life circumstances and privilege (or lack thereof).

Rest is a concept that, although biblical, Christians often do not embrace. In *Rest Is Resistance*, Tricia Hersey teaches us that "resting is an embodied practice and a lifelong unraveling. It is not something that can be trendy, quick, or shallow. Resting is ancient, slow, and connected work that will take hold of you in ways that may be surprising."[2]

Embracing rest and slowing down (my body and my mind) was the only option for me after my stroke and brain surgery all those years ago. Honestly, I would have chosen any other way. I learned quickly that I had no real experience with purposeful rest and no grasp of what embodied spirituality meant.

It was shocking to me that this busy mom (with a toddler at home) who was used to working, volunteering, and socializing had lost her multitasking ability. Life as I knew it shifted drastically; it went much slower. And while rest was indeed a foreign concept, I quickly learned to rest in God's presence. Have you ever had an experience that forced you to slow down?

Recently, I reflected on and lamented about this mistaken longing to juggle too many tasks with a wise spiritual friend. As she listened, she told me, "What a gift this experience of forced slowing down was for you all those years ago! You know true rest!" And I realized she was right. Why would I give up the gift of slowing down and learning to rest to begin rushing with the rest of the world again when I know how that feels in my body and spirit? I now know there are tangible benefits to focused presence and embodied living. I now know I can live into my calling and still find rest. Living in this way takes practice and discipline, but the rewards are bountiful. Twenty years after my stroke and brain surgery, meditation and naps help me continue to slow down each day, spend time with God, and embrace the gift of rest. I pray this book has offered you the gift of rest with Jesus. How will you embrace and embody rest beyond these pages?

26
radiant light

Read reflectively: John 9:1-7

True Blindness

Walking down the street, Jesus saw a man blind from birth. His disciples asked, "Rabbi, who sinned: this man or his parents, causing him to be born blind?"

Jesus said, "You're asking the wrong question. You're looking for someone to blame. There is no such cause-effect here. Look instead for what God can do. We need to be energetically at work for the One who sent me here, working while the sun shines. When night falls, the workday is over. For as long as I am in the world, there is plenty of light. I am the world's Light."

He said this and then spit in the dust, made a clay paste with the saliva, rubbed the paste on the blind man's eyes, and said, "Go, wash at the Pool of Siloam" (Siloam means "Sent"). The man went and washed—and saw.

ponder this

Consider the power of Jesus to bring physical and spiritual healing to us today and the question of suffering and its connection (or, better yet, nonconnection) to sin. What if we invited the transformative nature of encountering Jesus to change us today?

guided meditation

When you are ready, settle into your chosen posture, then center yourself with your breath. Next, imagine a radiant light surrounding you. This light represents God's presence and boundless love for you. With each breath you take, visualize this light growing brighter and more vibrant, like a bright, golden sun. Pause with this imagery and allow it to grow before you proceed.

Now use your imagination to feel God's divine light gently caressing your skin as God's love embraces you. Let this light and love fill you with warmth and comfort, knowing that this light is a tangible expression of God's boundless love for you.

See the divine light of God rising up your spine as you inhale. Then imagine that light traveling down your spine as you exhale, noticing any sensations.

Continue this pattern of inhaling the imagined light up your spine and exhaling the light down your spine. Repeat for several breaths.

With each breath you take, imagine God's energy flowing brighter and bolder, nourishing and restoring you. Feel the goodness of God fill you as this light syncs with your breath, saturating every cell of your body.

As you become more immersed in God's light, feel a sense of peace and restoration fill you.

Now, holding on to the imagined light of God within, reflect on a moment in your life when you experienced God's miraculous work. This may be an event, an encounter, or a situation that felt divinely guided. What miracle have you seen, heard of, or experienced?

As you relive this experience, allow yourself to reawaken the emotions and sensations associated with it. Let the awe, gratitude, and joy you felt during this miraculous moment fill you now.

If you can think of more than one moment, then reflect on each of them, one by one, as if you're watching a movie of your life. God's miraculous work is all around you, shaping your life beautifully.

Say to yourself: *God's light is within me, and God's miraculous work is always around me.*

Slowly breathe in and out as you reflect on the beauty of this reality.

soak in silence

Pause in the quiet and breathe purposefully. What do you sense?

for reflection

1. Which miraculous event or events did you see in your mind's eye?

2. Where has God been present and working in your life recently?

3. Do you need Jesus to make a special healing paste for your eyes today?

sensory cue

If today is sunny, go or gaze outdoors and bask in the light. Notice how the light allows you to see the world around you. Notice what the light feels like on your skin. Absorb the warmth of the sunlight and welcome it on your entire being. If the outdoors are not accessible or it is cloudy, close your eyes and imagine the warmth of the sun on you. Notice how this makes you feel.

closing prayer

Jesus,

Let me see your light clearly in my memories and my everyday life. Help me see your miracles and reflect your light to those I encounter this day. Amen.

27
simple calling

Read reflectively: Luke 9:1-5

Keep It Simple
Jesus now called the Twelve and gave them authority and power to deal with all the demons and cure diseases. He commissioned them to preach the news of God's kingdom and heal the sick. He said, "Don't load yourselves up with equipment. Keep it simple; *you* are the equipment. And no luxury inns—get a modest place and be content there until you leave. If you're not welcomed, leave town. Don't make a scene. Shrug your shoulders and move on."

ponder this

Jesus empowers his followers to proclaim the Good News. He asks his disciples to continue his ministry of healing and love, offering salvation and wholeness to those who believe. He tells them they have everything they need to accomplish this task and asks them to keep it simple. Consider God's calling in your own life as you enter this time of reflection.

guided meditation

Take a moment to settle into the quiet. Listen for the stillness around you as you breathe. Allow your body to relax. Release any tension or tightness you may be holding on to as you shrug your shoulders up and then release them down and away from your ears.

Now bring your attention to your breath. Take a deep inhale through your nose, noticing your lungs filling with air, and then allow for a long, audible sigh, letting go of any worries or distractions. Repeat by taking a breath in and then allowing for a long sigh. Listen to your own sighs as you release the breath from your body along with any thoughts that need to be freed from your mind.

For the next several breaths, when a thought or concern arises, return your attention to the sound of your exhale. Notice what it sounds like to let go in God's presence as you sigh.

In this present moment, you already have everything you need to connect with the healing and wholeness that God has gifted you. Allow yourself to embrace this truth as you clear your mind and pause. Hear God whisper, *You have everything you need.*

You may notice that your mind starts to wander. It is natural for thoughts to arise during times of centering; do not be discouraged. Acknowledge the idea without judgment, and gently bring your attention back to your breath, welcoming a clear mind.

If thoughts continue to arise, imagine a window in your mind. Open the imaginary window and free the thoughts that are distracting you.

Take a few more moments to immerse yourself in the quiet.

Say to yourself: *I have everything I need.*

Carry this sense of clarity and connection to God with you throughout the day.

soak in silence

Pause in the quiet and breathe purposefully. What do you sense?

for reflection

1. Do you feel centered and grounded in your life with Christ? If not, what small step could you take today to move you toward that feeling?

2. Are there circumstances or people you need to move on from to continue on God's healing path?

3. Do you believe that you have everything you need for your healing journey? Why or why not?

sensory cue

The posture of bowing down before God is referred to often in Scripture. This simple act is a reverent outward expression of one's inner devotion to and respect for God. It is also a wonderful posture to help us practice listening.

As you are able, find a version of a child's pose by kneeling on the ground with your knees hip-width apart. If this posture is not accessible, see the alternative below.

Take a deep breath and exhale slowly, allowing your body to

relax. Lower your torso forward and bring your forehead down to the ground or a prop (a blanket or block). If accessible, extend your arms forward, palms facing down, or relax them by your sides. Rest your buttocks on your heels, feeling a gentle stretch in your lower back. Relax your shoulders and let them drop toward the ground. Take slow, deep breaths, letting your body settle into the pose.

As an alternative to moving to the floor, lay your head and arms out on a table in front of you, then rest your head on your arms as you release onto the table as it holds your upper body. Stay in this simple child's pose (or variation) as long as it feels comfortable and soothing; release and let go with each breath. Listen for God as you bow down before the one who calls you.

When you are ready to come out of the pose, slowly lift your torso, bring your hands back to your sides, or support yourself on your hands, then slowly rise back up to a kneeling or seated position. Listen to your body and adjust the pose to ensure your comfort.

closing prayer

Healing God,
Please help me not overcomplicate my discipleship journey with you.
Meet me in the simple and miraculous practice of following you today.
I let go of what gets in the way and listen for you.
Amen.

28

forgiveness and compassion

📖 Read reflectively: Luke 7:36-48

Anointing His Feet
One of the Pharisees asked [Jesus] over for a meal. He went to the Pharisee's house and sat down at the dinner table. Just then a woman of the village, the town harlot, having learned that Jesus was a guest in the home of the Pharisee, came with a bottle of very expensive perfume and stood at his feet, weeping, raining tears on his feet. Letting down her hair, she dried his feet, kissed them, and anointed them with the perfume. When the Pharisee who had invited him saw this, he said to himself, "If this man was the prophet I thought he was, he would have

known what kind of woman this is who is falling all over him."

Jesus said to him, "Simon, I have something to tell you."

"Oh? Tell me."

"Two men were in debt to a banker. One owed five hundred silver pieces, the other fifty. Neither of them could pay up, and so the banker canceled both debts. Which of the two would be more grateful?"

Simon answered, "I suppose the one who was forgiven the most."

"That's right," said Jesus. Then turning to the woman, but speaking to Simon, he said, "Do you see this woman? I came to your home; you provided no water for my feet, but she rained tears on my feet and dried them with her hair. You gave me no greeting, but from the time I arrived she hasn't quit kissing my feet. You provided nothing for freshening up, but she has soothed my feet with perfume. Impressive, isn't it? She was forgiven many, many sins, and so she is very, very grateful. If the forgiveness is minimal, the gratitude is minimal."

Then he spoke to her: "I forgive your sins."

ponder this

Time around a dinner table evolved into a time of forgiveness. Consider how often Jesus invited transformation like this during a meal. Jesus invites all of us to understand the transformative power of forgiveness and to recognize our need for it. This woman knows her brokenness and so does Jesus. She seeks redemption and compassion for herself from her Savior. Her actions express her faith in Jesus and his willingness and ability to forgive her mistakes and transform her life.

guided meditation

Take a full breath in and a long breath out to center yourself. Notice the natural rhythm of your inhalation and exhalation. Feel the gentle rise and fall of your belly with each breath. Allow your breath to anchor you in the present moment, letting go of any distractions or thoughts that may arise.

Imagine yourself taking a bite out of a food that has gone bad. What does it taste like when it hits your tongue? What message does it send to your brain and your body? As quickly as you can, remove the awful flavor from your mouth by spitting out the food. Now imagine taking a few sips from a fresh, cold glass of water, washing the yucky flavor from your mouth.

Take a moment to recognize any negative thoughts, judgments, or criticisms you may be holding against yourself. Acknowledge the pain or discomfort that may be present in your body or spirit due to these thoughts.

Now release these negative sensations as you did the awful taste in your mouth. Imagine the yuck leaving your body. Just as you welcomed a fresh, cold glass of water, now you can welcome the gift of compassion. Feel yourself settle into compassion with each passing moment of quiet.

Say these affirmations to yourself:

I am human, and I make mistakes. I forgive myself for shortcomings and failures.
I welcome God's love, compassion, and forgiveness.
I release any judgments or criticisms I hold against myself.

Allow these affirmations to resonate within you. Sense the weight of self-judgment and self-criticism lift as you offer yourself the same kindness and compassion God offers you.

Take a few more deep breaths, inhaling God's forgiveness and the gift of self-compassion and exhaling any remaining tension or self-doubt.

soak in silence

Pause in the quiet and breathe purposefully. What do you sense?

for reflection

1. As you welcome God's grace and compassion, ponder this: Is there a habit, mistake, or sin you long to hand over to God today?
2. Do you practice self-compassion? If so, how? If not, what is one small step you can take today that will move you toward this practice?
3. When does negative self-talk arise in you, and how can you replace those words with God's words?

sensory cue

Mealtimes can generate deep and transformative conversations. Around the table with a friend or family member, bring up the topic of self-compassion. Share one way you are being kinder to yourself and notice if this sparks confidence, curiosity, or conversation.

closing prayer

Loving God,

Thank you for your forgiveness, redemption, compassion, and grace. Amen.

29
don't be afraid

Read reflectively: Matthew 17:1-8

Sunlight Poured from His Face
Jesus took Peter and the brothers, James and John, and led them up a high mountain. His appearance changed from the inside out, right before their eyes. Sunlight poured from his face. His clothes were filled with light. Then they realized that Moses and Elijah were also there in deep conversation with him.

    Peter broke in, "Master, this is a great moment! What would you think if I built three memorials here on the mountain—one for you, one for Moses, one for Elijah?"

While he was going on like this, babbling, a light-radiant cloud enveloped them, and sounding from deep in the cloud a voice: "This is my Son, marked by my love, focus of my delight. Listen to him."

When the disciples heard it, they fell flat on their faces, scared to death. But Jesus came over and touched them. "Don't be afraid." When they opened their eyes and looked around all they saw was Jesus, only Jesus.

ponder this

The transfiguration of Jesus reveals his divine glory and confirms his identity as the beloved Son of God. It invites believers to recognize Jesus' divine nature and to respond to his teachings with awe and obedience! Sit in awe as you welcome Christ's presence.

guided meditation

As you settle into your space, imagine yourself on a mountaintop in the presence of Jesus, only Jesus. Feel his loving embrace and imagine him so close that you sense his breath upon you now.

Jesus' eyes are filled with understanding, and his presence exudes a profound sense of peace. You feel warmth, kindness, and unwavering support.

Pause and be with Jesus for a few more breaths.

Hear the words of Jesus as spoken to the disciples and allow them to be breathed on you by him now: "Don't be afraid."

Now breathe these words in for yourself:

Don't be afraid.
Don't be afraid.
Don't be afraid.

These words, simple yet profound, carry a timeless and universal message. They remind you that no matter the circumstances, you are not alone. You are held, loved, and protected by God.

Listen closely. Hear Jesus whisper your name.

He wants to offer you what he offered the disciples, not to be afraid. Be receptive to the message on that mountain.

As you listen, you may hear something like:

I am with you.
Release your worries.
You are never alone.
Stay close to me.
Do not be afraid.

Pause now and open yourself to these or any other words God may be breathing on you in this moment.

Say to yourself: *I am not afraid.*

Take a few moments to meditate on the words Jesus said to you during this time. May they continue to comfort you.

soak in silence

Pause in the quiet and breathe purposefully. What do you sense?

for reflection

1. Is it easy or hard to imagine Jesus breathing on you and speaking your name today?

2. Can you think of a moment in your life when it felt like Jesus was near you—as close as your breath?

3. Has there ever been a time when you felt God's Spirit on you and fear or worry left your body?

sensory cue

Take three deep breaths, then say the words you heard from Jesus aloud to yourself, preferably in front of a mirror. If you are struggling to find the words, use one of the examples above.

closing prayer

Lord,
Help me breathe in your presence always and not be afraid.
Amen.

30
freely and lightly

Read reflectively: Matthew 11:28-30

The Unforced Rhythms of Grace
[Jesus said,] "Are you tired? Worn out? Burned out on religion? Come to me. Get away with me and you'll recover your life. I'll show you how to take a real rest. Walk with me and work with me—watch how I do it. Learn the unforced rhythms of grace. I won't lay anything heavy or ill-fitting on you. Keep company with me and you'll learn to live freely and lightly."

ponder this

Jesus longs for us to find rest and relief from weariness and burdens through relationship with him. Jesus presents himself as the source of rest and the solution to our spiritual heaviness. He extends an invitation to all who are weary to come to him and experience true rest for their souls. Jesus offers this invitation of grace and the promise to companion you in a life that feels lighter.

guided meditation

Find a quiet and comfortable place to sit or lie down. Read these words, then soften or close your eyes and take a deep breath in. With your extended exhale, let go of any tension or worries, welcoming a free and light feeling within your body. Consider placing a hand on any part of your body that feels tense, stressed, or burdened. Breathe purposefully into this part of yourself. Pause until you are ready to move on.

Now imagine you are near an ocean at sunset. You are not alone beside the ocean; Jesus is near. Begin by focusing on the image of Christ as you continue with slow, steady breaths and long, extended exhales.

As you breathe, notice the ocean's waves, rhythmic and unforced. See how they move toward you and away from you, beginning to sync with your own breath. Pause as you breathe with the waves.

Feel the ground beneath your feet. You are anchored to the earth as the sunset fades to moonlight. Jesus is near and takes your hand to keep you company with the setting sun. Feel his touch and breathe with the waves. Notice how being in this place with Jesus feels inside your being. Pause until you are ready to move on.

Now imagine yourself walking with Jesus along the ocean in the moonlight, freely and lightly.

Pray: *Jesus, I release my burdens.*

Breathe with the waves as you imagine your burdens being carried away to the depths of the ocean. Pause until you are ready to move on.

Jesus keeps you company as you savor and enjoy the moonlit walk and the refreshment this time with him provides you.

As you return to the present moment, you are refreshed from your time journeying with Jesus.

soak in silence

Pause in the quiet and breathe purposefully. What do you sense?

for reflection

1. When was the last time you experienced burnout? Which aspects of your life feel exhausting in the current moment?
2. When do you rest? How do you rest?
3. How do you keep company with Jesus?

sensory cue

At some point in your day, come to a reclined posture in which you can be supported by the earth, your bed, a chair, or the floor. In yoga, this reclined posture is known as our final resting pose or savasana. Settle the back of your body into whatever is supporting you. Feel your body touch what is beneath you and sink down. Invite your insides to relax. Finally, invite the top of your body to release and settle toward the back of the body. Next, soften your entire being, from the top of your head to the tips of your toes. As you allow gravity to hold you, relax and release any striving or strongholds (physical or emotional). Imagine being held by God's everlasting love and care for you.

closing prayer

Jesus,
Show me how to keep company with you. Help me live freely and lightly.
Amen.

sensing our way forth

*But all shall be well, and all shall be well, and
all manner of thing shall be well.*
JULIAN OF NORWICH (CA. 1342–CA. 1416)

You have experienced the healing waters with Jesus as your companion. You have opened your hands to both receive and release. You have felt God's energy and light on you. You have imagined and moved and breathed with the Holy Spirit in a variety of ways!

On this journey, you have been invited to spend time with God by engaging your senses and your whole being through reflection with Scripture, imagination, mindfulness, movement, and breath. What a journey of presence we have been on together! The beautiful thing is that the refreshment you experienced in these pages was already within you. God gave you the ability to sense the Spirit's presence. We may not walk with Jesus physically, but we are grateful that he walked before us and that he walks with us still today.

The passages, meditations, and prompts in this book invited you closer to God, but you are the one who met with God in these pages using your very own body. This closing invitation is just as important as the journey we have been on, so try not to rush ahead, but keep sensing and savoring on this embodied journey with Jesus as your guide.

Years ago, I was teaching a class in which I used a phrase you have also read in this book: *You have everything you need.*

The words of Jesus to his disciples inspired this phrase. In my class, we used these words as part of a breath-prayer affirmation in that the attendees were to breathe in *Thank you, Lord* and then breathe out *I have everything I need.* One of my students contacted me later to tell me that her mother had been very ill and that she had been so worried about the days ahead and what this would mean for her and the decisions she had to make—until we prayed that prayer. Those words shifted her heart and mind to remember that God had equipped her with everything she needed for that situation, and she sensed that all would be well.

Hear this: You have everything you need to continue your healing journey with God!

Our bodies were created miraculously. We tend to be the ones who put them down and discount their abilities and ignore the cues they give us. We get frustrated with them much more often than we praise them for miraculously facilitating our breath and life each day.

But what if, from this point forward, you journey forth with the confidence that God has given you everything you need to live a present and embodied life with your Creator? Imagine how that simple acknowledgment might feel for each of your days on this earth. I am ready and willing to commit to this journey of presence with you; I already have. It does not mean you or I will always get it right but that we welcome the invitation to live an embodied life each day.

I have done a lot of healing work in my adult years, yet I still have much work to do on this journey. But friends, God has given me everything I need. And God has given you everything you need too.

As we close this book, we have only just begun to grasp what it is like to live fully embodied in the present moment with God—with our whole selves! Living in a more embodied way may change how you see the world or interact with Scripture. Yet there is no finish line. Instead, there is an invitation for your life. God is with you in every breath! How will you live your "with-God" life?

As Trappist monk Thomas Merton wrote, let us "be all alive, body, soul, mind, heart, spirit. Everything must be elevated and transformed by the action of God, in love and faith."[1] Bring your whole self close to God, and you will be transformed.

> YOU HAVE EVERYTHING YOU NEED TO CONTINUE YOUR HEALING JOURNEY WITH GOD!

It is really important to note that while this embodied journey is for you, it is also for others, even if we have not entirely figured it out. Your willingness to live into a more embodied spirituality gives others permission to do the same, seeing the action of God in your life and theirs.

We can and should sense, notice, and embody the love and faithfulness of Jesus and as a result share them with others through our daily lives.

Will you use your imagination one more time? Envision God's light shining over you again now. Feel it warming your body, seeping into every pore—filling *you* with light.

Now imagine that light shining from you and out into the world. Ah!

As God's perfectly imperfect people today, we are called to fully receive God's love, faithfulness, and light and reflect them for the world to see. The world needs the love, faithfulness, and light of Christ. You are a light for Christ that shines his Spirit into the darkness and invites others to experience God's love and care. What a gift.

inspired intentions

We are invited to be ever present with God. Yet we may not always sense God's presence if left to our own words. So, as we close, I invite you to combine your words with God's through these positive affirmations.

Ponder these words, and use them as breath prayers or affirmation statements. I embrace both in my daily life (there is a list posted in my closet that has been there for years) and find them especially helpful on my journey. You already repeated affirmations in our times of meditation. Use the following to help you carry forth your mindfulness practice with intention. Consider hanging this list in your own closet or posting it on your computer screen, dashboard, or bathroom mirror.[2] Or make your own list.

Say to yourself:

I am a light, called to share God's love.
(inspired by Matthew 5:14)

I am loved unconditionally.
(inspired by John 3:16)

I am learning and growing.
(inspired by Matthew 28:18-19)

I live an abundant life.
(inspired by John 10:10)

I am called to be a peacemaker.
(inspired by Matthew 5:9)

I am filled with joy.
(inspired by Luke 2:10)

I let my light shine.
(inspired by Matthew 5:16)

I believe.
(inspired by Mark 11:23)

I serve.
(inspired by Mark 10:43)

I am never alone.
(inspired by Matthew 28:20)

I am filled with God's peace.
(inspired by John 14:27)

I show compassion.
(inspired by Luke 6:36)

I am reminded that with God nothing is impossible.
(inspired by Luke 1:37)

I have everything I need.
(inspired by Matthew 6:25)

Notice if one affirmation stands out more than another after you have soaked in these Gospel-inspired intentions. Hold on to those words, and breathe them in and out as I leave you with one final invitation.

closing with gratitude

To honor this time with God, you are invited to create a thank-you letter to Jesus for your body and how it serves you on this journey with God. If you don't consider yourself a writer, don't panic! This letter can take many different forms. You could

- record an audio version of your letter,
- make a list of things that come to mind,
- create a piece of art,
- capture a portrait, or
- find another way to express thanks to Jesus for your body.

No matter which format you choose, I urge you to capture your gratitude for the miraculous body that lets you sense Jesus near you today. Recognize its importance on your spiritual journey with your Creator. And remember to embrace God's love for you.

In Hillary McBride's insightful book *The Wisdom of Your Body*, she concludes with a letter to her body.[3] Her letter inspired me, and while it feels vulnerable to share in this way, I close this devotion with a letter of gratitude for my perfectly imperfect body, written to the Human One, Jesus. I invite you to do the same to honor your embodied journey with your Creator, God.

Dear Jesus,
Thank you for teaching me what it is like to live in a body. Thank you for going slow enough to allow me to reach for the hem of your garment over and over. Thank you for holding my hand as I welcome your healing waters upon me—over and over. Thank you for living in the present, speaking the truth, and loving everyone always.

Thank you for giving me a body that senses, feels, and loves.

What a gift the senses are to me!

I love smelling pine trees in the mountains, fresh flowers in the garden, and the ocean's salty air.

I adore tasting homegrown vegetables and the love that made them grow.

I long for the warm embrace of my spouse and a giant hug from my grown son, who towers over me.

I appreciate seeing the colors of a glorious sunset and watching the day fade away into night.

I am comforted by hearing church bells in my backyard.

I welcome seeing the caring smiles of friends and companions.

I am overcome that I get to sense your presence in the wind, the waves, and the sunlight, but in my body most of all.

I appreciate that you help me catch my breath whenever I feel overwhelmed by the troubles in this world around me.

I get goose bumps when your Holy Spirit stirs within me.

I feel your energy flow through me when I rest in your presence, and I am so glad your Spirit is alive in me today. I do not ever want to take your presence for granted.

I know I have taken my body for granted. It makes me sad that I often forget to use my senses to sense your presence. I wish that I did not speak before listening so often. I regret being tempted to talk negatively about myself, yet I hear you reminding me "I am here. I am with you. I see you. I love you. I forgive you. I know you."

I do not always act like it, but I am grateful for the way you made me and how everything about me draws me close to you.

I appreciate that you created me with a bubbling imagination and a creative mind. The gift of being an Enneagram Four means it is natural for me to dream, feel, imagine, and sense. What a gift it is to help others do the same with you.

I love the miracle of the body you gave me. I even appreciate my popping knees because they have carried me far and helped me see great sights with you.

I embrace the wavy hair, neither curly nor straight, that changes with the weather and reminds me that no two days are the same on this journey with you.

I am learning to love this body that changes size and shape in various seasons of life. I hear you remind me that I am strong. I am wise. I am living my life dependent on you in times of change and reminded of one certainty: All things change, myself included.

I am grateful this body gave birth to a son, now a remarkable adult.

I am sad but thankful for your presence during the loss experienced with an unborn child, which first taught me what grief feels like.

I am glad for the sometimes on-key and sometimes off-key alto voice that does more than sing songs in worship or the car. I am glad you have given me a voice to speak the truth for myself but mostly for others.

I am humbled for the ears you gave me to hear stories of your miraculous presence and the complex challenges we all face and to be a safe receiver for many. These ears hear more than stories; they hear your voice whispering often, and that is a gift I long to cling to more often.

I am so happy there is breath in my lungs, which means I have another day and hopefully many more birthdays on this earth to journey with you.

I never take for granted your gift of peace.
I am grateful.
I am grateful.
I am grateful.

I have your breath in my lungs. Jesus, the embodiment of God's Spirit, your healing touch is on me and oh so welcome.

Thank you for helping me go slow and allowing me to sense your presence every step of the way, even in the storms of life. Thank you for making me who I am. Thank you for reminding me that I have everything I need because of you.

Love,
Whitney

bonus content

Practicing presence helps us embody God's Spirit within us. If you found these guided meditations helpful on your journey with God, return to them often and share them with others.

You can find additional downloads and resources and listen to these meditations at

whitneyrsimpson.com/withGodineverybreath

and find additional guided prayers and meditations at

exploringpeace.com/podcast

acknowledgments

With wholehearted gratitude . . .

Every great writer I know says the following, but it is true. There is not enough room in this part of the book to name every person who supports my spiritual formation and writing journey. From friends, family, and students to directees, peers, mentors, and coworkers—I am truly grateful for your companionship and your trust. Not every name is on this list, but if you're reading this, I am grateful for you.

Here are just some of the people who have shaped this particular book and the invitation it offers you, dear reader.

Peace Seekers, podcast listeners, retreatants, students, directees, and *you*, the reader who supports my creative work and trusts me to accompany you on your journey: I start by saying that I am humbled; thank you.

Troy Simpson: Always my best friend, you believe in me and encourage me to "disappear" and unplug to get this creative work from my heart and my head onto these pages; thank you.

Dwight Judy: Your teachings, mentorship, and books have been the most practical and relational tools for my journey. I am beyond grateful for your investment in me and my call to ministry; thank you.

Beth Booram: You have listened to all the ups and downs on

the path and nudged me to always stay true to my "with-God" life; thank you.

Mary Irby: I am forever thankful you said yes to being my yoga teacher. You have taught me so much about embodiment and encouraged me to use my voice and lean into my own gifts; thank you.

Stephen Handy: You offer safe space to heal and help among God's people, and you have helped me "dare to shift" again and again and again; thank you.[1]

Mary Anne Akin: What fun God is that I gained a mentor and friend like you, who encourages me to always listen to God and who was the one who listened to every one of these words before they were printed—what an abundant blessing; thank you.

Kasey Hitt: If you had not first invited me into that boat with Jesus, I may never have known the gifts of spiritual direction and guided meditation as I do now; thank you.

Jo Reese: I miss you. You helped me better understand the gift of energy and Jesus; thank you.

Tracy Schenk: From grocery shopping to plate making and sunshine soaking, you know how to be God's hands and feet; thank you.

Leighanne Fulmner: You not only taught but modeled resting in God and helped me embrace meditation even when I did not always want to. Here we are twenty years later, my friend; thank you.

Jill Fisk: I am so grateful for a spiritual friend who reminds me that multitasking is not a superhero quality but presence is; thank you.

Jane Murray: From my first trusted student to teacher and everything in between, goodness, I am so glad Jennie said we were destined to be connected—we are; thank you.

Dana Trent, Kristen Vincent, and Sharon Seyfarth Garner: It makes me giddy to have writing friends like you! What a treat to cheer one another on. I am so glad for the giggles, for

ACKNOWLEDGMENTS

your friendship, and for our time in peer group over the years; thank you.

Deborah Sáenz and David Zimmerman: I truly enjoyed that cup of tea together on Music Row. I was honored by your belief in me and my creative work from day one. Partnering with everyone at NavPress has been a sensory delight. Deb, your story shaping and book edits have made this devotional more beautiful; thank you!

Elizabeth Schroll: Thank goodness for an efficient copyeditor like you. I am so appreciative of every detail we corrected or considered, helping this devotional come to life; thank you!

The Tyndale marketing team: You are doing the hard work of getting this book out into the world; thank you.

Christa Laub: You make my life easier by handling all the tasks that make the *Exploring Peace Meditations* podcast possible; thank you.

Eugene Peterson: Although you are no longer on this earth, I am so grateful for how you help us engage with Scripture today through *The Message*. Your words continue to shape my life with Jesus; thank you.

Bono: Wow, you get it. Yes, I am thanking you, a rock star I have never met, in this devotional book. I adore your work and the good energy and light you shine from afar; thank you.

The Order of Deaconess and Home Missioner, all my siblings serving in outside-the-box ways while representing the United Methodist Church: Keep doing what God called you to do; thank you.

Our church family, campus community, and Wesley students: It is so good, right, and fun to do life with you in community; thank you.

Hey, God: I never imagined the healing path my thirty-first birthday would have led me on. I'm so thankful for your companionship with each new step; thank you.

about the author

Whitney R. Simpson's writing encompasses her passion for embodied spirituality and the ministry of spiritual formation. As a soul-care practitioner, she has served in many roles, ones that often overlap. From yoga teacher to spiritual director to campus minister, she longs to help others reach their fullest human potential as they explore the gift of God's peace. She is the author of *Holy Listening with Breath, Body, and the Spirit* and *Fully Human, Fully Divine: An Advent Devotional for the Whole Self.*

As the founder of Exploring Peace Ministries, Whitney hosts a free prayer and meditation podcast and offers contemplative retreats and ecumenical spiritual-direction sessions as well as yoga and meditation workshops.

Whitney began practicing yoga as part of her recovery after a stroke and brain surgery in 2005. She was hesitant to believe that a yoga practice could ease her chronic pain, but embracing the practices of yoga and meditation have been foundational for her healing journey and her soul-care work. These days she enjoys taking walks with the family dog, reading historical fiction, soaking up the beauty of the great outdoors, and learning to empty nest with her spouse as they watch their son find his passion and purpose as a young adult.

After many years of yoga practice, Whitney is now an

ABOUT THE AUTHOR

Experienced Registered Yoga Teacher (E-RYT 500). Before completing her first yoga-teacher training, she pursued the two-year Professional Certification in Spiritual Formation at Garrett-Evangelical Theological Seminary. Whitney currently serves as Wesley Fellowship's campus minister at her community's local university. As a deaconess in the United Methodist Church, she is an advocate for peace and human equality, longing to create safe space for all. She considers it an honor to hold space for you to meet God through embodied spirituality and the ministry of spiritual formation. You can listen to *Exploring Peace Meditations* or discover the Exploring Peace community at exploringpeace.com. You can also find free bonus content for this book and connect with Whitney directly at WhitneyRSimpson.com.

notes

INTRODUCTION
1. Henri J. M. Nouwen, *The Wounded Healer: Ministry in Contemporary Society*, 2nd ed. (New York: Image Doubleday, 2010), 69.
2. See, for example, https://www.nccih.nih.gov/health/meditation-and-mindfulness-what-you-need-to-know.
3. Aundi Kolber, *Try Softer: A Fresh Approach to Move Us out of Anxiety, Stress, and Survival Mode—and into a Life of Connection and Joy* (Carol Stream, IL: Tyndale Momentum, 2020), 13.

EMBODIED LIVING
1. Celeste Snowber Schroeder, *Embodied Prayer: Harmonizing Body and Soul* (Liguori, MO: Triumph Books, 1995), 15.
2. W. David O. Taylor, *A Body of Praise: Understanding the Role of Our Physical Bodies in Worship* (Grand Rapids: Baker Academic, 2023), 45.
3. Stephanie Paulsell, *Honoring the Body: Meditations on a Christian Practice* (San Francisco: Jossey-Bass, 2002), 10.
4. Hillary L. McBride, *The Wisdom of Your Body: Finding Healing, Wholeness, and Connection through Embodied Living* (Grand Rapids: Brazos Press, 2021), 19.
5. B Grace Bullock, "Present-Moment Awareness Buffers the Effects of Daily Stress," *Mindful*, March 15, 2017, https://www.mindful.org/present-moment-awareness-buffers-effects-daily-stress. Also see Crystal Goh, "Your Breath Is Your Brain's Remote Control," *Mindful*, February 16, 2017, https://www.mindful.org/breath-brains-remote-control.
6. Amanda Blake, *Your Body Is Your Brain: Leverage Your Somatic Intelligence to Find Purpose, Build Resilience, Deepen Relationships and Lead More Powerfully* (Trokay Press, 2018), 46.
7. Blake, *Your Body Is Your Brain*, 47.
8. Blake, *Your Body Is Your Brain*, 53.

NOTES

9. Gregory A. Boyd, *Seeing Is Believing: Experience Jesus through Imaginative Prayer* (Grand Rapids: Baker Books, 2004), 16.
10. Kevin O'Brien, *The Ignatian Adventure: Experiencing the Spiritual Exercises of Saint Ignatius in Daily Life* (Chicago: Loyola Press, 2011), 141.
11. Dan Harris and Jeff Warren with Carlye Adler, *Meditation for Fidgety Skeptics: A 10% Happier How-to Book* (New York: Spiegel & Grau, 2017), 4.
12. Bessel A. van der Kolk, *The Body Keeps the Score: Brain, Mind, and Body in the Healing of Trauma* (New York: Penguin Books, 2015), 102.
13. For more on big-*T* Trauma and little-*t* trauma, see Danielle Carr, "Tell Me Why It Hurts: How Bessel van der Kolk's Once Controversial Theory of Trauma Became the Dominant Way We Make Sense of Our Lives," Intelligencer, *New York*, July 31, 2023, https://nymag.com/intelligencer/article/trauma-bessel-van-der-kolk-the-body-keeps-the-score-profile.html.
14. Christine Valters Paintner, *The Wisdom of the Body: A Contemplative Journey to Wholeness for Women* (Notre Dame, IN: Sorin Books, 2017), 38.
15. Thomas Keating, *Invitation to Love: The Way of Christian Contemplation*, 20th anniv. ed. (London: Bloomsbury, 2012), 105.

INTERLUDE | WHY *THE MESSAGE* BIBLE?

1. *Bono and Eugene Peterson on the Psalms*, conversation facilitated by David Taylor, Fuller Studio (Fourth Line Films, April 26, 2016), 21:43 https://fullerstudio.fuller.edu/bono-eugene-peterson-psalms, 10:21.
2. *Bono and Eugene Peterson on the Psalms*, 15:20.
3. Octavia F. Raheem, *Pause, Rest, Be: Stillness Practices for Courage in Times of Change* (Boulder, CO: Shambhala, 2022), 18.

INTERLUDE | WHAT DOES IT MEAN TO BE WHOLE?

1. See Richard J. Foster with Kathryn A. Helmers, *Life with God: Reading the Bible for Spiritual Transformation* (New York: Harper Collins, 2010), 37.

12 | FORGIVENESS AND GRACE

1. John Newton, "Amazing Grace" (1779). Public domain.

14 | SHARED LIFE FORCE

1. See, for example, Kirsten Nunez, "What Are the Advantages of Nose Breathing vs. Mouth Breathing?," *Healthline*, February 1, 2021, https://www.healthline.com/health/nose-breathing; "Nose Breathing Lowers Blood Pressure, May Help Reduce Risk Factors for Heart Disease," American Physiological Society, January 17, 2024, https://www.physiology.org/detail/news/2024/01/17/nose-breathing-lowers-blood-pressure-may-help-reduce-risk-factors-for-heart-disease?SSO=Y.

INTERLUDE | SAVORING THE SCRIPTURES
1. Whitney R. Simpson, *Holy Listening with Breath, Body, and the Spirit* (Nashville: Upper Room Books, 2016), 24.

INTERLUDE | CONNECTING WITH GOD
1. Evelyn Underhill, *The Essentials of Mysticism and Other Essays* (London: J. M. Dent & Sons, 1920), 2.

24 | PROPHETIC PRESENCE
1. *Rûaḥ* and *pneuma*; see Blue Letter Bible, accessed November 23, 2024, "Strong's H7307—*rûaḥ*," https://www.blueletterbible.org/lexicon/h7307/kjv/wlc/0-1 and "Strong's G4151—*pneuma*," https://www.blueletterbible.org/lexicon/g4151/kjv/tr/0-1.
2. See, for example, Shilagh A. Mirgain and Janice Singles, "Progressive Muscle Relaxation," US Department of Veterans Affairs, last updated May 1, 2024, https://www.va.gov/WHOLEHEALTHLIBRARY/tools/progressive-muscle-relaxation.asp.

INTERLUDE | EMBRACING THE GIFT OF REST
1. Cole Arthur Riley, *This Here Flesh: Spirituality, Liberation, and the Stories That Make Us* (New York: Convergent Books, 2022), 38.
2. Tricia Hersey, *Rest Is Resistance: A Manifesto* (New York: Little, Brown Spark, 2022), 17.

SENSING OUR WAY FORTH
1. Thomas Merton, *Thoughts in Solitude* (New York: Farrar, Straus and Giroux, 1999), 15.
2. You can visit whitneyrsimpson.com/withGodineverybreath for downloads of these affirmations.
3. Hillary L. McBride, *The Wisdom of Your Body: Finding Healing, Wholeness, and Connection through Embodied Living* (Grand Rapids: Brazos Press, 2021), 255–258.

ACKNOWLEDGMENTS
1. Michael Bowie and Stephen Handy, *Dare to Shift: Challenging Leaders to a New Way of Thinking* (Knoxville, TN: Market Square Books, 2023).

NavPress

Bold. Loving. Sensible.

Since 1975, NavPress, a business ministry of The Navigators, has been producing books, ministry resources, and *The Message* Bible to help people to know Christ, make Him known, and help others do the same.®

"God doesn't want us to be shy with his gifts, but bold and loving and sensible."
2 Timothy 1:7, *The Message*

Learn more about NavPress:

Learn more about The Navigators:

Find NavPress on social media: